WANDER LUST

WANDER LUST

THE CHOCOLATE MADE ME DO IT

DEVON WERNER

NEW DEGREE PRESS

COPYRIGHT © 2021 DEVON WERNER

All rights reserved.

WANDER LUST

THE CHOCOLATE MADE ME DO IT

ISBN   978-1-63730-674-1   *Paperback*

         978-1-63730-763-2   *Kindle Ebook*

         979-8-88504-101-0   *Ebook*

"*The only person you are destined to become is the person you decide to be.*"

—RALPH WALDO EMERSON

*To my sister, Donna, your unconditional
love and unwavering support has created
a foundation for all of my success. To my
MuNchKin, Lauren, your independence, resilience,
and world travels inspire me every day.*

*In memory of my strong, sarcastic, loving mom,
not a day goes by when you are not on my
mind and in my heart. And my laid-back, belly
laughing, comedic brother-in-law, Ray. You
both are loved and missed beyond measure.*

*And to my bright-eyed, mohawk-sporting,
extraordinary son Matteo, you are the absolute
love of my life and by far my most incredible
adventure. May you have the courage and curiosity
to craft a story that fulfills your wildest dreams.*

CONTENTS

AUTHOR'S NOTE

—

Dear Readers,

What if you woke up one day in a hospital bed without the physical capacity to take care of yourself? Would you have regrets? Would you be disappointed with your story?

Lori Gottlieb, best-selling author, therapist, and speaker, gave a TEDx Talk in 2019 entitled "How Changing Your Story Can Change Your Life." In it, she challenges us to ask ourselves what we want our story to be and then tasks us to go write our own masterpiece. I never knew just how much her words would resonate with me until I made the decision to write this book.

I knew I wanted to chronicle my travels and adventures as a keepsake to remind me of who I was and what the world was teaching me. I thought for sure that my journey would lead to a metamorphosis. That I would come out on the other side an entirely different being, similar to the apprehensive caterpillar emerging from its cocoon with the iridescent glow of butterfly wings. What I had not accounted for were the forces of the universe that would alter my course time and time again, taking me through the highest of highs and the lowest of lows. Life is unpredictable, but the lessons that stem from those low moments are transformative. We're constantly changing and learning.

In life, we often have a picture of what we think the future will look like. A picture that is so clear to us that we can embrace it as if it has already come into existence. So what do we do when we become so attached to a vision of how things should be that we lose sight of how things are? What do we do when we are scared to alter our current course for fear that it will change our future?

I spent a year of my life in such an interesting juxta-position. Most of my days were grounded by my work in the hospital intensive care unit, but every month, I would coordinate my time off and head out on some once-in-a-life-time experiences.

One year.

Nine countries.

Fifteen adventures.

Each of these journeys paved the way to recognition of my true self and set me on a course that introduced to me to the love of my life. When I decided to write this book, I knew the ending, I knew the story… My story would tell of my world travels, my self-discovery, and my happily ever after with the woman of my dreams. I would share this evolutionary tale in a way that paralleled the great triumphs and love stories etched in ink and bound tightly together on the bookshelves that surround me.

Speaking of those love stories, one of my favorites—*Eat, Pray, Love*—chronicles the journey of Elizabeth Gilbert, famed author and memoir writer, as she goes through her own journey of self-discovery, which ultimately ends with her falling in love. This epic fairy-tale ending won over the world, so much so that in 2010, Ryan Murphy adapted her best-selling memoir for the big screen under the same title. The image of that final scene is vividly ingrained in my mind. Gilbert, portrayed by the vibrant Julia Roberts, stands waiting at the end of the dock before the camera pans to a view of her and the Brazilian businessman she fell in love with heading off into the sunset.

Most people may think the story stops there, but that is simply not true.

In a 2016 Facebook post entitled "Me & Rayya," Gilbert took to social media to disclose that she and her husband had separated and that she was in a relationship with her female best friend, who at the time was battling a terminal cancer diagnosis. Being a gay cisgender female author with a vested interest, I had followed Gilbert's story closely over the years: her separation, her coming out, her love story, and the profound impact of her loved one's death. I thought about how her story changed significantly since that moment at sunset on the dock in Bali. I thought about how the ending that won the world over was actually just the beginning of a different story. I suspect it was a story that was inevitably filled with so much more than she could have envisioned.

My dear readers, I realize now that the book I thought I would write is not the story that needs to be told.

Life doesn't always have to culminate with a love story.

For a hopeless romantic, this is a very hard realization to have. All the books, the movies, and the fairy tales teach us otherwise, but what we often overlook is what happens next. After Gilbert had what she thought was her "happily ever after" on the dock in Bali, she went on to find a love greater than she ever could have imagined, only to end up once again her own. I do believe it is possible to have more than one great love, and I also believe it is possible to find joy and fulfillment in other ways. Maybe it's as simple as escaping the ordinary.

Take a moment to evaluate your day. Is it filled with draining people, boring routines, and an overwhelming desire for more? What if you stepped outside of your ordinary day-to-day and tried something different? Sure, it's easy to dream about, but there are a million reasons why we just keep on keeping on. When we sit with our excuses and spend so much of our days living out the monotonous moments, we start to become acclimated to that life, and in turn, all we can do is long for more. We often forget what it feels like to experience something new. However, when we alter the course, each moment becomes something more impactful. It changes our perspectives. It changes us. We become someone different. We learn to appreciate life's unpredictable ways, and we embrace the story we choose to write.

I offer this story to those of you who might want to know about the chapters that you don't always get to read: the ones that come next. The true happy ending comes in the realization that you are worthy of an epic story, regardless of what has been written before. That even a broken version of yourself can still have joy and happiness if you are willing to let go of the excuses and fear that hold you back when you decide to stop trying to just live life but instead try to *be* life.

We always have a choice to live by the excuses or to live despite them. Take this book, for example. There are many reasons for me not to write this… it's too unfinished, too exposing, too uncomfortable, too soon. If I have learned anything on this journey, it's that there will always be people reminding you of the reasons not to. Let me be the one to say that it's okay to be a little selfish. And with that, I have decided to press forward with this book, to grant myself permission to let my vulnerability write for me, to open the door to reflection and healing, and to emerge on the other side with whatever grace and wisdom the words on the paper are willing to offer us all.

There is a quote often attributed to Gandhi: "Be the change you want to see in the world." Is that possible? While the concept sounds great, I think that I would much rather be the change I want to see in myself.

Reflectively yours,
Devon

PROLOGUE

It is now six months since my epiphany and rebirth. I am sitting at the wood-grained desk in my office, having just finished putting the last touches of my story into words. I reach over to the pieces of chocolate that sit beside my half-empty coffee cup. I pause, staring at these pieces before selecting one to partake in. I begin to unwrap the metallic foil around the smooth piece of dark chocolate and place it in my mouth as a means of sweet reward after closing out that last chapter. As I push the last bit of that decadent morsel onto my tongue, I smooth the edges of the foil to reveal the most serendipitous message…

"Read the last page first."

Touché chocolate, touché.

PART 1

THE WANDER

—

CHAPTER 1

AND SO IT BEGINS

——

"You must live in the present, launch yourself on every wave, find your eternity in each moment. Fools stand on their island of opportunities and look toward another land. There is no other land; there is no other life but this."

—HENRY DAVID THOREAU

In eleventh grade English Lit, I was introduced to the penned words of a literary mastermind. A man who understood the value of nature, equality, and experience. His writings were monumental in the movement of *Transcendentalism*. What is that? Well, to paraphrase the wonderful *Encyclopædia Britannica*, it is a philosophical movement based on a belief in the essential unity of all creation, the innate goodness of humanity, and the supremacy of insight over logic and experience for the revelation of the deepest truths. It was this idea that in order to understand reality, you must experience reality. I was utterly captivated by this philosophy. At sixteen years old, I was being told to cease merely living and begin to "*be.*" I thought to myself, *I'm going to do it. I am going to live the best life, travel the world, seize the moment and just "BE."* It seems my sixteen-year-old self did not really understand what that meant.

As I grew older, I discovered more about this concept: the idea of experiencing life through my own personal perspective and finding meaning in those experiences. I have learned to *live deliberately* and recognize the value in every serendipitous moment.

Cut to April 2018, a month that seemed to remind me of the things I had missed out on in life.

I was sitting there, going through some papers in my safe, and I came across my passport… only to open it up and find it expired last year, April 2017. This couldn't be right—I had had my passport for over ten years and not a single stamp? Seriously! How disappointing, and a little sad, to be frank. How was it that in ten years' time, I had not traveled the world like my sixteen-year-old self had envisioned? But it was okay, right? Life happened. WAIT A MINUTE! What happened to that whole idea of not living life but *BE-ing* life?

I'm a single woman. I can't travel alone. I have no one to go with me. It's too expensive. I don't have the time. I'll go when I'm older, etc., etc., etc. This was not acceptable. I had a list of excuses as to why I had not experienced the world, but the truth is, they were all crap. The list could go on for days, but the reality is they were just excuses that stemmed from fear. But fear of what?

I would sit and listen to my niece talk about her cool experiences traveling through Europe, and I would watch my sister post pictures of Ireland, Mexico, and Cuba. And

I would sit there and say, "Wow, that looks cool, I want to travel one day too." What was I waiting for?

I remember sitting at work on a Saturday morning in the ICU when we had a string of evaluations come through. Three of my evaluations were under the age of forty, all with massive strokes. Now granted, working in a hospital, I am predisposed to seeing many of worst-case scenarios, and I recognize that what I see is not entirely reflective of the general population, but it got to me… what if I woke up one day in a hospital bed before the age of forty without the physical capacity to take care of myself? Would I have regrets? Would my sixteen-year-old self be disappointed that I never experienced the adventures this world has to offer? It got me thinking.

No more excuses.

I am not getting any younger, and there is a world full of amazing experiences out there, just waiting for me.

I had been contemplating some travel for a while, but I was still a bit nervous to actually go through with it. Then, as if the universe just knew that I would talk myself out of it, it gave me a sign… by way of chocolate. I opened my little piece of Dove chocolate (dark sea salt and caramel, yum), and the inspirational message on the foil said, "Book the flight." And so, I did! I mean, the chocolate told me to do it, so I had to, right?

I booked my first trip to the Dominican Republic. I mean, can we say paradise! I was beyond excited and looking forward to spending some time enjoying the sun, sand, and sangria. The cool thing was, one of my best buds, who I had not seen in over a year, decided to book a flight to the Dominican Republic as well. What better place to catch up with an old friend than under an umbrella on a white sandy beach? I had a feeling the shenanigans would be endless, and I anticipated there would be some great stories to share as the travels unfolded.

"How vain it is to sit down to write when you have not stood up to live."

—HENRY DAVID THOREAU

Touché, Mr. Thoreau!

I couldn't just live through one experience, so I went ahead and booked some more.

Once the traveling commenced, I thought I would continue to follow Thoreau's example and literally chronicle my journey in a travel blog. If my first entry was any inclination as to how this year of adventures would go, it was sure to be a wild ride.

Travel Blog Entry August 2018

So here I am, waiting to board my first international flight, and what better way to take advantage of my time than by writing my first travel blog? Brought to you by the good folks at Washington Dulles airport and the crew of United Airlines. I am currently sitting here in the D terminal, enjoying warm soup (it's a bit cold in here) and a bottle of water.

Today started off well. I woke up a few minutes before my alarm and got myself dressed and out the door on time. Upon arrival at the Greensboro airport, I unloaded my bags and headed to security. Made it through without a hitch—minus being told my passport was invalid. I had a brief moment of panic before being told I needed to sign it to validate it, and with a swift scribble of the pen and a few minutes to let my heart rate ease back down, I was good to go! The flight was smooth, and despite the rain on the ground, the views in the sky were breathtaking. Thanks to seat preference, I was able to snap a few shots from the window seat before settling into the music on my headphones.

Once we landed and the plane came to a stop in DC, we stepped down the ladder steps and onto the tarmac before heading into the terminal. The brisk breeze was a little bit of a surprise. After getting into the terminal and over to my next gate, I was informed that the plane was slightly delayed for some mechanical issues. That's when it got interesting. Initially, it was just a thirty-minute delay, which ideally would have been perfect because that would have put me in Punta Cana at the precise time my friend's flight from Atlanta would be landing. They got us all set, lined up, and ready to start boarding. All good to go, boarding began... but wait, just kidding. Then we were deboarding, and our flight was delayed again. This time for a few hours, as the aircraft was deemed not safe to fly, and therefore we needed to wait for a new aircraft to fly in from Florida.

Now, I don't know about you, but if someone tells me an aircraft is unsafe to fly, my response is surely: "Okay, thank you very much. I will wait for the safe plane, please." To my shock, that was not quite the response amidst the group. Now trust me, I get it. You have vacation plans, maybe going to a wedding, going to see family, or maybe flying home… but are any of those events really going to matter if your plane disintegrates over the ocean because some do-hickey on the whatchamacallit stopped working? I was just as disappointed as the next girl, I promise you, but I also had a lot of plans in my life that I wanted to be around for, including all of my upcoming travel adventures. Plus, I was pretty sure my sister would be pissed if I wasn't around to enjoy Finland next year.

What was even crazier than the frustrated individuals begging to get on a broken plane was the way they were reacting to the poor women at the desk, who were thrown into the lions' den like a fresh steak. I mean, really, people, they were just doing their jobs. I am pretty sure none of those women woke up that morning thinking, "Man, today would be a great day to cancel some flights and really screw with people." These women went above and beyond to answer questions, relay information, and arrange for snacks, water, and meal vouchers.

Just when you think the pack couldn't get any more aggressive to these ladies, imagine what happened when the printer broke halfway through the alphabetical printing of the vouchers. Now, these gate agents could have snapped. In fact, they had every reason to—but they held their composure throughout. With my name bringing up the rear of the alphabetically ordered list, I was able to sit back to the very end of this chaotic process and just watch everything unfold.

There was one gentleman left in front of me. As he reached the desk, he asked how he could go about contacting customer service. Now, if you are a people watcher, you may have seen this "type." The type of guy that looks like he is reaching his boiling point, pacing quietly as he stalks his prey, filling with frustration and rage, tension building… and it was about to happen. He was about to go in for the kill.

And then… he proceeded to take down each gate agent's name and thanked them for all of their hard work and courtesy. He told them they had handled things exceptionally and that his desire to contact corporate was merely to compliment them for their work. What a powerful moment to witness. Kindness in its truest form. These ladies, who were surely stressed-out at this point, gained this sense of calmness. I, too, smiled and thought about the way the morning had just unfolded and how a little bit of kindness and positivity changed things.

Now I am sitting here on the floor, typing away on this laptop, feeling grateful. One, because I am sitting here awaiting my flight and not falling out of the sky trying to put on an oxygen mask or secure a flotation device. And two, I'm going on a trip to paradise, a trip I have been very much looking forward to. And three, I've got a chocolate cookie.

I am sitting here, smiling and content, knowing I'm going to have a good trip and a lot of fun. I am choosing to look at the good in this experience, because seriously, who wants to let a little three-hour delay ruin all the fun that is in store? Sure, I could be angry, frustrated, miserable… but where is that going to get me? What is that going to do, aside from putting a sour taste in my mouth at the beginning of this whole travel experience? Nah, I'm not down for that.

There are a lot of times in life where it is easy to get caught up in the frustrations of a situation: at work, at home, on the phone with the cable company, etc. But I have learned firsthand that it is really hard to change your mindset once you go off the deep end and that nothing good comes out of those emotions. So instead, I am choosing to smile, be happy, have some patience, and see the good in whatever happens. It's not always easy, and I let my emotions get the best of me sometimes too, but when you are given the opportunity, take a minute, look around and ask yourself, "What really matters?"

Now, on to paradise!

The trip itself was filled with a plethora of pleasant surprises and opportunities to really think about what matters. For the first time in as long as I could remember, I found myself living each moment with a degree of intention that my life had been lacking. Paradise became a state of mind, brought to life by the endless white sandy beaches, luscious tropical foliage, clear blue water, beautiful weather, and the lingering scent of Mama Juana, an alcoholic drink unique to the Dominican Republic. According to the locals, it's made from rum, red wine, honey, tree bark, and herbs. It's also considered an aphrodisiac. I could go on and on, but I will try to keep my fawning in check.

Being new to this "world traveler" thing, there was an immense element of the unknown going into this trip. I did not know what to expect or how it would be for me in a foreign country. I learned so much about myself during this trip.

In my element, I'd like to think that I am very outgoing and friendly (others may just say talkative and loud). However, in a new environment, outside of my comfort zone, I am the exact opposite. I am an introverted-extrovert. The thought of going outside my comfort zone is terrifying to me. So just imagine my anxiety over being thrown into the mix of a foreign country, surrounded by new people, speaking words I don't always understand… let's just say the thought of cowering under a palm tree with a book and some music for four days was surely an option. Luckily, my buddy Cassidy had decided to join the trip, so I would at least be spared that level of anxiety for this initial international experience… right?

So, it turns out… not entirely the case. While my previous experience was limited to domestic vacations, I learned at a young age when traveling with friends, you must understand that there will be times where you may want to do different things. I am absolutely on board with that. Spending too much time together can lead to tension, and I have found that the best travel partners are the ones that you don't have to entertain twenty-four seven, and yet when you are together, you can still live it up and have a blast. But I have never had to worry about that on foreign soil. Until this trip, and as evidenced by one of the funniest moments of our travels together.

Cassidy had gone up to the room to take a nap, but I wasn't tired, so I decided I was going to push myself out of my comfort zone and head to the pool/bar for a bit—by myself. After all, this whole travel experience was supposed to open me up to new things. But let's be real, that walk from the room to the pool was filled with an immense level of social anxiety. The scent of chlorine began to grow stronger as I approached the pool. The sudden rumbling of my stomach, combined with the intense degree of perspiration, was reminiscent of my experience as the new kid in school. By the time I got to the pool deck, my heart was beating louder than the bass echoing from the DJ booth, my palms were sweating, and my brain was sending signals telling my body to run and hide. I was so ready to retreat to my palm tree in isolation.

Instead, I put down my bag, mustered up some semblance of courage, and hopped in the water. I waded over to the bar for a strong drink and, in what I can only envision as this tiny Piglet-like voice stuttered the words "hey there, where are you from" to a group of people up by the bar. The introverted voice inside my head was screaming out—*RETREAT!* Just then, a voice from the crowd responded, announcing the group's origins.

"They're from Canada, I'm from Cleveland, and those two are from New York." After that, the conversation flowed so easily. Over the course of the next two hours, I found myself lost in conversation with so many awesome and fun individuals from all over the world. I also was a part of an intense round of flip cup that spanned eighteen people deep. By the time my friend Cassidy returned to the pool, my new friends were chanting my name and sliding me down the "soapy slide" bar. It was an absolute blast!

Over the next few days, we spent a good deal of time hanging out with the group we had met that day. During the day, Cassidy and I would head out on excursions and then make our way back to the pool by late afternoon for what became an understood meeting spot for the crew. By the time the trip came to an end, I'd made some incredible connections with some cool people who I planned to meet up with and see again in various places around the world. From the Canadian boys who volunteered to show me around Montreal, to the incredibly fun physicians from Puerto Rico, the nursing student and his brother (also a nurse), and everyone else, it was truly eye-opening to how genuinely nice people can be.

I have learned a few invaluable lessons from this first travel experience.

The first: be kind. It can make a difference. Whether it's a rough day at the airport or a stranger that approaches you to say hello, most people you encounter are inherently good. Sometimes, if you take a moment to get to know their story a little bit, you might be surprised at how much you have in common.

The second: we can be our own biggest barrier to new possibilities, but if we can recognize that and are willing to step outside of our comfort zone just a bit, we might be surprised to see how much we were holding ourselves back from truly LIVING life as a participant rather than being a spectator.

The third: don't open your mouth when swimming in a cave! Montezuma's revenge is no joke! (thanks, Cassidy, for the Gatorade, banana, and Imodium) Luckily, he was nice enough to hold his revenge until the last night!

My advice, don't let your fear stand in the way of your fun, push yourself out of your comfort zone, and don't be afraid to say hello; you might just meet some amazing people!

CHAPTER 2

SEPTEMBER REFLECTIONS

"The best journeys answer questions that in the beginning you didn't even think to ask."

—JEFF JOHNSON

Gazing out the window of my home office on a dreary, wet Autumn day, I found myself daydreaming about some of my upcoming adventures. In preparation for those travels, I had joined this travel app that connects world travelers. Wow, to even think I could be considered among the likes of such. Me, a *world traveler*—I liked the sound of that. To say I was excited would be an immense understatement. I was pretty sure Amazon appreciated my enthusiasm, given all of my camera and travel gear purchases!

I was still new to the whole idea of traveling and often wondered what I would learn over the course of the next year. Sure, there are the basics: *sign your passport, don't drink the water, don't swim with your phone,* etc. All of which were incredibly valuable lessons to learn on my first adventure, but I was curious to learn more. I remember seeing the posts of my fellow world travelers and was mesmerized at what the world had to offer.

When I started thinking about traveling for a year, I knew where I wanted to go but had never really stopped to think about where the world would take me. Would I be the same person I was before I started it all? Well, I could already answer that. No! Even after one experience, I felt like my perspective had changed. I realized very quickly how humbling it was to see what a small space we occupy in this world and how much there is out there to experience. As I started making reservations, my bucket list consisted of a handful of places I wanted to see, but with each new adventure booked, the wish list grew exponentially.

I started thinking a lot about who I would meet over the course of the year. It was crazy to think that my circle of friends had already started to expand across borders and oceans. Just that morning, I was messaging with one of my friends from the Dominican Republic trip, and I couldn't wait to finalize plans to see them again! Just as I was excited for all the new people that I would meet, I was also looking forward to reconnecting with friends that I had not seen in a while. Later that month, I was set to reconnect with an old friend at Disney World. The happiest place on earth! Did I mention we were set to meet during Epcot's World of Nations Food and Wine festival? A great opportunity to do some "market research" for my upcoming travels.

I planned that trip on a whim; it was last minute and only for a day. Yes, that's right: one single day.

You may be wondering why I would choose to cram all of that into a single day. Well, the answer is simple—because that was all the time I had, and I wasn't going to say no.

Well, okay, maybe it was a little more complex. This trip was planned in the spur-of-the-moment. The conversation went a little something like this. Phone beeps, and it's a text message from my dear friend Leiselle, who had lost her father last year around this time. Message reads:

> Want to go to Disney with me the weekend of
> September 28th through the 30th? My Dad's birthday...

Enough said. Trip booked for twenty-four hours in Disney because, well, unfortunately, I get it.

After having lost my mom right before I started graduate school and then my brother-in-law, Ray, shortly thereafter, Leiselle was my saving grace. She helped me through one of the worst periods of my life, so being able to provide a fraction of that support to her was the least I could do. So, to Disney, we would go.

When I started this year of *yes wandering adventure*, I said to myself that I was going to be more open to the experiences that the universe throws at me. I was NOT going to let myself overthink and talk myself out of the opportunities that presented themselves. Now granted, not every opportunity will work out, but I was going to make sure I said YES, a little more often and not let the excuses prevent me from doing the things I want to do.

NO EXCUSES had become a mantra for me. I thought about everything that was going on in the world around me. Then and now. This past weekend, our coast was hit with a pretty devastating hurricane; I thought about the people who lost their homes, personal belongings, and security in an instant. It reminded me that we often find ourselves bogged down by stress, materials, and life in general. It's easy to get so caught up in it all and lose sight of the beauty and comfort we can find in our experiences and in the memories that cannot be washed away. Life can be harsh at times and leave us feeling like we are ill prepared, out of control, and downright uncomfortable.

Traveling became my way of embracing the chaos and searching for what the world has to teach me. It was an opportunity to see past the stressors of life and find something more valuable than any item on my shelf. A way for me to grow in my own skin and find security in the space that exists outside of my usual day-to-day.

I did not know exactly what the next year would hold. I was not sure of the lessons I would learn, the people I would meet, or the person I would become… but as I sat and contemplated it all, the possibilities intrigued me. I was looking forward to the many adventures ahead and seeing all of the things I may not have known to look for.

Speaking of things, I may not have known to look for… did you know that Disney has "Hidden Mickeys"?

"What are Hidden Mickeys," you ask? According to a September 2017 article on Tripster.com by Anne Mercer, Hidden Mickeys are subtle silhouettes that are strategically placed throughout the theme parks by Disney Imagineers. You can usually find them in decor, rides, or areas where Mickey Mouse would not usually be found. The post goes on to explain these originated because Epcot did not want to associate characters with the alcohol that was being served in that park. Hmm, maybe I should investigate this whole concept further.

Disney in a Day

What a weekend. Actually, I should clarify that by saying what a day! Yep, that's right: Disney in a Day! A single, fun-filled, laughter-filled, food-filled, friendship-filled day. What an absolute blast! From Disney's Magical Express to Chef Mickey's for a little food and fun, a relaxing hotel room at Coronado Springs, traveling the "World" with beer, wine, margaritas, and mimosas, and ending the night with some great music and a bunch of new memories. What more could you ask for in a day!

I have been fortunate enough to have experienced the magic of Disney on several occasions over the course of my life. I've seen it with the eyes of a crazed teenager during a senior trip in high school. As a coach, I've stood under a flurry of confetti, placing gold medals after my girls won the Wide World of Sports Disney Showcase tournament. I've kept the beat as a drummer that marched down Main Street USA in a Disney parade. And on several occasions, I have walked through these parks with the likes of friends bundled in winter coats and family members burnt from the intense sun and heat. That place holds a lot of great memories for me. But that day in Epcot with my friend Leiselle brought back some extra special ones.

> "May Más Tiempo Que Vida"
> translates into
> "There is more time than life."

This quote was taken off the wall inside San Angel, a quaint little hidden gem located in the heart of Mexico at Epcot's World of Nations. Of all the places and magical spots that exist within this world, this is one of my favorites. As you walk in to escape the blazing sun (and it was definitely blazing that day), you enter a perpetual twilight marketplace filled with vibrant smells and bursts of color.

As you wind yourself down the ramp into the market, you can peer deep through the crowds, and you might cast your gaze upon a stunning replica of the Mayan ruins alongside an erupting volcano cast into the starlit skies. And, every so often, you hear thunderous clouds roar as the sky gives off the illusion of lightning—as if it were playing connect the dots from star to star. It really is a cool place, and the food is delicious.

When you enter, you are greeted by colorful skeletons and "deathly" creatures. Then, as you turn your gaze to the wall, you will see this quote: "There is more time than life." Part of the mystical theme of the attraction is its recognition of the Mexican culture's celebration for the Day of the Dead.

Given why Leiselle and I came to Disney in the first place, I couldn't help but be taken aback by the literal writing on the wall in the middle of this Day of the Dead themed attraction. But now, what is there to make of it? I couldn't help but have a little internal chuckle as I read an article on Imbibe entitled "Day of the Dead Drinking Traditions" by Emma Janzen that said, "We drink to honor the deceased." Ha, nailed it! We'd had our fair share of drinks (thank you, Epcot Food and Wine festival).

In current practices, which date back to the ancient Aztec and Toltec civilizations, there is this idea that death was not something to be mourned but rather recognized as a continuum of life. In time with the fall harvest, these cultures hold extraordinary festivities centered around the concept of welcoming spirits back to the realm of the living to celebrate, dance, and dine alongside us (we held up our end of the deal by doing the same; although, our singing probably chased a few spirits in the opposite direction). In Mexican culture, "Final Death" occurs when there are no memories left of our loved ones or friends—but as long as memories live, our departed family and friends remain alive and with us (Janzen 2017). This was an oddly comforting sentiment.

As I sat at the airport waiting for my flight home, I reflected on the words and the day. I couldn't help but think of my own memories. Part of the reason I love this place, and in particular, this attraction, was because I remember the first time I went. I must have been maybe twelve years old or so. My sister and brother-in-law brought me with my niece when we were kids. It was one of the highlights of our many family vacations. Ray was like a second dad to me, and he absolutely loved the place.

I remember walking around the bazaar area, exploring all of the trinkets and colorful ghostlike odds and ends. "Dev watch out," he would joke while tapping me unsuspectingly on the opposite shoulder with the arm of a plastic skeleton. I remember the soothing comfort of the air-conditioned boat ride housed within the attraction to offer respite from the Floridian heat waves. I remember the erupting volcano that echoed through the hollowed-out dining area. I also remember that every subsequent trip back to Disney, we always went to that same restaurant. Between the food, the cool conditions, the mystical environment, and the memories, it was a family favorite.

Staring at that wall of words, I remembered Ray. Just as I'm sure my friend was remembering her dad.

It's funny, you know, the moments and signs you get when you are not intentionally looking for them. I have found that

they actually exist everywhere. And when you see them, you
feel this universal connection. It's like the ones you care about
are right there, hanging out on your adventures. The (very
literal) writing on that wall also helped to remind me that
life, in its physical form, is short, and we owe it to ourselves
to make the most of the time we get to live it.
So…
Drink the wine.
Eat the chocolate.
Book the flight.
Embrace the memories.
Take a moment to read the signs and remember those who
will always be right there with you.

CHAPTER 3

JUMPING FOR JOY

———

How do we go about finding joy in our experiences when it looks like things are not going our way?

When I planned my October trip, I had this grand idea of what it would be like to visit Canada in the fall. Walking around Toronto in a nice comfy hoodie, enjoying a fresh cup of Tim Horton's coffee, and taking in the scenic views of vibrant foliage as I ventured around the outskirts of the city itself. I pictured sitting at a table in the Distillery District among the hustle and bustle of people heading to their next outdoor engagement. I envisioned taking the ferry over to the islands to catch the views of the skyline at sunset with nothing more than a light jacket to break the wind off the water. My ideal image of Canada at the peak of my favorite season: Fall. While this postcardlike vision manifested in my mind, you can only imagine the potential disappointment that would ensue as I read the headlines of the Toronto weather website just a few days before my trip.

"Toronto's weather is so terrible right now that it's even colder than Alaska," and, "Rain, cold, wind and then some more rain," and the best one yet, "Winter weather predicted for the weekend."

Say what? Oh yes, it wasn't a joke. It appeared Mother Nature had kindly decided that I needed a little more preparation before my February trip to Finland by way of skipping Fall and moving right into Canadian winter. Nevertheless, I was too excited for this solo adventure to abandon ship.

So, less than twenty-four hours from my trip, I was walking out of Starbucks with a steaming hot latte and a delicious chocolate cake pop into the cold, wet rain pouring over North Carolina. For a second, I thought to myself, *Ugh, this is* not *fun.* I feared it would only be worse that weekend.

Then, just as swiftly as that thought entered my mind, my attention was quickly diverted. This tiny handsome little boy with navy-blue sneakers and a gray sweater came into my line of sight. His mom walked next to him with her hands firmly wrapped around her coffee and the boy's hands almost an identical match around his tiny cup of hot chocolate.

I imagined if I had a son, this would inevitably be how we would spend our mornings as well.

In that instant, almost as if serendipitous, the young boy lowered his body deep into a crouching position, flexed up his knees, and then forcefully propelled upward, lifting his body off the ground, and then just as swiftly came back down to meet it with a loud splash. Droplets of water fired out in all directions. Then, the boy let out this bellowing laugh. You know, the kind that echoes through the air and becomes contagious and energizing. At that moment, all I could think was *touché young fella, touché!* The joy resonating from that boy was evidenced by his enormous grin as he continued this activity all the way down the sidewalk en route to his mom's car.

At that moment, I realized that with a little flexibility and preparation, I too could experience the joy I was so much looking forward to. So, on my way home, I stopped at probably the only ski shop in existence anywhere near me and purchased a few new items of clothing. I told the owner a little bit about my trip and my need for winter clothing. He was so incredibly nice, and while assisting me with my shopping, he proceeded to tell me the story of a stuffed rabbit's desire to become real through the love of his owner—more popularly known as *The Velveteen Rabbit* by Margery Williams. Now, mind you, I had heard the story before, so I wasn't quite sure where he was going with it until I reached the register.

You see, the young stuffed rabbit lives in a little boy's nursery with all his other toys. Over time, the rabbit quickly becomes forgotten amongst all of the shiny, new toys that the boy receives. Then one day, the boy's grandmother places the stuffed rabbit with the boy when he sleeps, thus rekindling the relationship. The story goes on to take a somber turn when the boy falls ill, and the family is directed to get rid of some of the boy's old toys, including the disheveled stuffed rabbit. But thanks to a little nursery magic, and the unwavering love and bond, the rabbit is rewarded with the opportunity to become real and live out his life among other real live rabbits (Williams, 2004). Truly a wonderful tale of love, loyalty, and magic.

As I continued to engage in dialogue with the shop owner, he explained to me that he had been running that shop for a long time. Occasionally, he told me, he looks out over the store and thinks of his items like the stuffed rabbit stuck in the box—just wanting to be loved and played with.

Truth be told, I was still a little confused about the metaphor.

My puzzled look must have been extremely obvious, prompting him to go on and explain, "This gear wants to go outside. It wants to play in the snow. It wants to go on adventures. It wants to be alive! So I'm going to knock off 30 percent because I don't want the price to be what keeps them from an adventure." Man, what a great guy!

Thank you, kind sir, for your time, your story, and your generosity!

So I was all ready to go. Mind you, the wardrobe was a bit different than originally planned, but I was just as excited, if not more, for the epic adventure. I intended to jump in the puddles, dance in the rain, and find joy everywhere I could. It might not have been exactly as envisioned, but I was beginning to think it would be better than I could have ever imagined.

Leading into the weekend, I thought for sure I would be incredibly nervous traveling completely solo, but as it turns out, it was more just sheer excitement. I woke up early, 3:30 a.m., and got myself ready for the day. I put on my comfy pair of black yoga pants and an oversized white hoodie, still with the softest fleece inner lining that hadn't quite been completely laundered away.

I have since decided this outfit will be referred to forevermore as my "lucky travel attire"—more to come on that.

I headed out into my garage and loaded up the car with my trusty carry-on suitcase and jam-packed book bag. After a few beeps of the alarm and the mechanical closing of the garage door, I drove off. It was a seamless trip to the airport, with no traffic (at 4 a.m.). Upon arrival, my day started with a steaming hot latte from Starbucks and an ever-so-smooth boarding process.

So far, so good.

Then, while sitting on the runway in line for takeoff, the pilot came over the speaker to announce they forgot to put fuel on one side of the plane. Glad they figured that out before we took to the skies! What I didn't realize was the process of fueling a jet is quite a lengthy one. Our flight would now be delayed by ninety minutes. Many people were quite upset due to connections. But I'd tried to commit to a go-with-the-flow process. Rather than being upset about my own missed connection, I figured I'd go with it and just stay on the plane while many others deboarded.

The next available connection for my carrier was not until 3:45 p.m., well after my original 9:30 a.m. connection. This would have put me into Toronto at 5 p.m., which would have been disappointing since I was only going to be there for two full days. I took a deep breath and searched for all other airlines leaving out of Michigan, my connecting airport. Turns out there was an Air Canada flight leaving at 10:30, which would still put me in Toronto by noon.

I calmly called the airline and asked if they could put me on the flight. Unfortunately, I was told this was not possible as they were not an associated airline. I stated I understood but asked very pleasantly if she could check with her manager just to see if there was any potential option and, if not, that it was okay. Before she even got back on the phone, an alert came through on my texts with an updated itinerary on the Air Canada flight! Awesome! I could relax for a bit on my first leg of flights. To top it off, I had a full row to myself, and the flight attendant gave me all three snacks and an extra water (remember this, it has an importance for later). Ha, but wait…

I arrived in Michigan with only thirty minutes to connect. I got off the plane with my carry-on and ran to the nearest monitor—*wait, what?* No listing for Air Canada. So, I asked for help only to learn a little fun fact about Detroit Metro airport. There are two different terminals, and in order to get between them, you have to go out of security, take a shuttle or a cab, and then go back through security! I now had twenty-five minutes to get out, catch a cab, get through security at an international terminal, and make it to the gate before the doors closed.

How fitting that for this trip to Toronto, I was inspired by none other than the couple that won *The Amazing Race Canada*. Now it was my turn to experience my own version of the amazing race.

I sprinted through the airport as fast as I could, hailed a cab who kept trying to convince me to wait for the free shuttle until finally realizing I was okay with paying the twenty dollars to go five minutes down the road. I paid him while en route, and upon arrival, waved thank you, jumped out of the cab, and broke into another high-speed foot race to security.

While approaching security, I saw the line was wrapped all the way around. At this point, I had to make a choice: continue my efforts to make the flight or just relax, head back to the original terminal, and take that much later flight.

My competitive side kicked in… I was going for it! I got in line with about fifteen minutes before they stopped boarding. I waited for two minutes to catch my breath before bending down to prepare my laptop and liquids. Just as I leaned down, a security guard tapped me on the shoulder and said, "Come with me." A little freaked out, I complied. He rubbed my hands with a special cloth and then scanned me with a wand and said, "Just put your bag on that empty conveyor and go ahead through, have a safe flight." I am not sure if it was just plain luck or if this security guard saw my complete state of desperation and decided to take pity on me. Either way, I'd

take it! I felt like I just experienced the adult equivalent of a
big win in Chutes and Ladders.

I smiled, said thank you, and to the belt I went. *I might
just actually make this flight after all!*

I glanced down at my watch. Ten minutes until the doors
close. I started prepping my body for what was about to happen. As I placed my bag on the conveyor belt, I began the
mental preparation for my mad dash to the terminal gate.

And then…

Just as my bag made its way through the metal machine,
the light flashed above the belt agent's computer and made
annoying buzzer sounds. It was very similar to the anxiety-in-
ducing buzz you hear when your tweezers hit the metal edges
of the surgical game Operation. Only this time, the anxiety
was exponentially higher as it was my bag screaming to be
searched. A slightly disappointing sense of defeat started to
creep over me as I worried that I would not make it in time.

Remember that free water from my first flight? I forgot
that I needed to throw it out since you can't take over three
ounces of liquid. Despite the delay, I was not ready to give up.
My heart was pounding, the adrenaline was pumping, and
with the water now in the trash, I had about three minutes
to go to the opposite end of the terminal. I'd come too far
to give up now.

I grabbed my bag, snapped the straps tightly around my
chest, and sprinted as fast as I could. I *needed* to get to that
gate. I seriously have never run for a finish line so hard in my
life. With each stride, I felt my chest grow tight. I could barely
breathe. My side was cramping. My legs were burning. Let's
be real. I was not in any shape for a foot race. As I rounded
the corner, I saw the gate come into my view. I just had to
go a little bit farther.

As I made my approach, I couldn't tell if the door to the jetway was open or closed. I got to the counter and could barely muster out a word when the attendant stated, "Welcome, Miss Werner." Followed by, "We have a ten-minute delay if you would like to use the restroom before you board." It was like music to my ears! I'd made it, and I could take a moment to collect myself (and locate the nearest defibrillator should I need it). I quickly FaceTimed my sister, Donna, because seriously, you can't make this stuff up. Also, because I needed her video surveillance just in case I passed out.

After a few minutes of recovery, I boarded the plane and made my way to my seat. Again, I was welcomed with an entire row to myself, followed by a smooth flight into Toronto and arriving only twenty minutes later than my originally planned arrival. I picked up my car and headed into the city.

What a rush, literally and figuratively! I'm not sure how things aligned the way they did, but in hindsight, it was quite entertaining and fun. I felt like the universe was supporting my journey and the rest of the weekend followed suit.

Riding the high of overflowing endorphins, I decided to take advantage of some incredible opportunities in Toronto. Within the first few hours of exploration, I found myself signing a release waiver for my life. If my heart survived the airport escapades, surely it could handle a little more adrenaline. What better way to test this theory than by strapping myself to the outer edge of a skyscraper 116 stories above the street? After a few minutes of safety videos, and some last-minute harness checks, I was hanging out over the edge of a five-foot walkway leaning into the same sky that my plane had just made a descent through not that long ago. Talk about an adrenaline high.

The next day, I decided to keep with the theme of heart

pounding, body rushes. I woke up early and made my way down to take in the sight of the iconic Niagara Falls. Sure, walking around the falls can take your breath away as you observe the beauty rising from the mist, but that seemed a bit tame compared to the previous day. In keeping with heightened experiences, I decided to get a bird's-eye view by way of zip line! I attempted to film the experience, but as the wind met my body head on, my jacket sleeve blew across the camera lens, leaving me nothing but complete blackness accompanied by the unique zip of cords and my joy-filled screams. This, of course, resulted in the ever-so-popular but quite overpriced purchase of the touristy photo and video footage from the Kiosk—the ones that are strategically placed right at the exit so that you cannot proceed by without a sales pitch.

A swipe of my card and one flattened souvenir bag later, I walked back to the car and made my way back to the city.

I decided to slow down my pace and spent the remainder of my time exploring Toronto's various neighborhoods. I enjoyed a delicious fried chicken sandwich at Mill Street Brewery in the Distillery District. This was washed down with a variation of the mouthwatering sour beers from some local craft breweries in Kensington. I finished off with dessert. I was informed that no trip to Toronto would be complete without indulging in the sugary goodness of a "Beaver Tail." Imagine a funnel cake that has been flattened like a pancake into the shape of a beaver's tail. It's then topped with whipped cream, banana slices, crumbled Oreo, cinnamon sugar, and chocolate. Yum!

After dessert, I made my way down to what the locals refer to as the "519" or the Canadian "Gay Village." I loved this area because it reminded me so much of my favorite spots back home in the gayborhood of Philadelphia. The usual Toronto street signs were accented with the bright colorful lines of the pride rainbow and, as you approached the walkway at Church and Wellesley, the pedestrian crosswalk was emblazoned with the same beautiful colors. There was something so inherently welcoming and calming to me. It's hard to explain how something as simple as a colorful symbol could induce such a sense of belonging, but it always has, does, and likely will for me.

I decided to top off the evening with a little entertainment at the local drag queen show. Between performances, I engaged in a delightful conversation over chocolate martinis with my new friends Chad and Mike. I mean, talk about the most adorable couple. They gave me some great advice for my upcoming travel adventures and even provided dinner recommendations for my trip to Montreal.

After I said goodbye to my new friends, I made my way back across town and settled into my lovely accommodations. Toronto was truly a ten out of ten.

Sometimes, things don't always go according to plan. In those moments, we must let ourselves remain flexible and adapt to situations that are beyond our control. We must remain resilient and, when there are components that we can control, we must be willing to tighten our laces and push ourselves beyond our comfort zone. We must let go of that negative mindset that can hold us back. It is really easy to hold tight to the things that don't go our way. Change in weather, change in plans, etc. Life needs to be more about finding the joy in all things. That weekend I found joy in the rush, in the calm, and everything in between.

The puddle can either ruin your shoes or it can make your day.

Oh, and in case you were wondering, my return flights were smooth and uneventful.

CHAPTER 4

FINDING THE HOLIDAY SPIRIT

The holiday season brings with it the opportunity to think about our lives in so many different ways, ways that can be unique to each individual. The season is built upon innate prompts that guide us through time with elements of gratitude, nostalgia, and reflection. Whether it is the smell of warm pumpkin pie wafting across the air from the kitchen or the familiar jingle of sleighbells that you hear in every other song, the holiday season is distinctly recognizable. So, what do you do when all of those prompts become heavy? When you just aren't quite sure that you're up for all the festivities? Sure, everyone loves the holidays, but sometimes the holiday season might not be as joyful as we might hope, and we just need a little space to figure out what we are ready for.

The holidays were always a big deal in my family. Big meals with enough sides to suit every palate, more noise than a crowded sports arena, a few dysfunctional family arguments, and the inevitable exhaustion that left family members strewn across the furniture. Growing up, the holiday season came with many holiday traditions, from making massive amounts of potato salad at thanksgiving, baking enough pies and cookies to induce a sugar coma, or waking up early for Christmas breakfast and then rushing over for dinner at my parent's house just a few hours later. That's right, dinner. My family always wanted to find a way to accommodate all of the various holiday commitments, from shopping plans to in-law visits and matinee movie dates with friends, etc. Apparently, the best way to do this was to eat a massive holiday "dinner" at twelve-noon with enough fixings to feed a small army. This was a time of year that I looked forward to as a kid, but after losing my mom and brother-in-law, the holidays just did not incite the same positive anticipation as they had in the past.

For the past several years, I'd done everything I could to avoid the holidays. I would pick up extra hours at work or just try to sleep away the days until the holiday passed. Those strategies were simply not going to mesh well with this new mindset of embracing discomfort and living life. So, instead, I wanted to find a way to honor my travel commitment but make room for whatever grace I mind need to extend myself. With that, I decided to start the holiday season off a little more subdued… or so I thought.

Knowing that holidays were a bit different now, I couldn't help but consider how refreshing it might be to just step away and do something a little out of the ordinary. I decided to trade in traditional turkey and dressing for some authentic Jamaican jerk chicken and dirty rice. Why not? Turns out this was a brilliant decision.

As November approached, I reached out to my friend Leiselle to see if she was interested in joining me for a trip to the Caribbean. Now, Leiselle is a friend that will always hold a special place in my life. She has been a beacon of comfort and a vibrant mixture of tranquility and liveliness with a side of sass. She has become a sister to me, and so she was the perfect sibling to enjoy the holiday with. She is also from the tropics, and who better to enjoy the sun and sand with than a true local? The goal was a quiet relaxing weekend on the beach with drinks in hand and lively vibrations of the Calypso drums ringing in our ears.

After just finishing up some intense weeks at our respective jobs, it was a weight-being-lifted sensation to arrive on the island of Jamaica with nothing to do but relax. We were greeted by the welcoming waves from the many palm trees that lined our route to the resort. Once we arrived and got settled in, we decided to focus our efforts on the goal at hand: *relaxation*. Over the course of our first few hours, I would say we were making solid progress toward said goal.

We spent some time poolside, where the warm sunshine altering the tone of my skin was a perfect complement to the ice-cold deliciousness of blue slushed libations being served up by the bartender. Leiselle spent time reading and relaxing in the lounger, and I intermittently set off to answer the calls of competition from the beach volleyball court. Did I mention that I am horrible at relaxation?

As the trip went on, we repeated these activities frequently, but in an attempt to change things up a bit, we decided to go on a "relaxing" catamaran cruise and indulge in a little snorkeling with about thirty of our newfound friends. We figured what better way to engage in some local activities than to jump in the gorgeous blue waters and explore the aquatic inhabitants? We put on our snorkel apparel and splashed into the crystal-clear abyss. The sights were incredible: from rigid points of the stingrays gliding across the sandy bottom to the soft flowing fins of angelfish floating above. There were beautiful mounds of coral and all of these bright illuminating colors crossing rapidly through our visual field. After about an hour of submerged investigation, we concluded our search for SpongeBob and hoisted ourselves back onto the boat for a little shoreline cruise.

Now, one thing they don't explain very well is how to prevent the water from coming into your snorkel every time you submerge. One of the side effects of this phenomenon is overindulgence in salty seawater. The apparent resolution to this is to dilute the salty taste with the sugary delicious-ness of more colorful drinks, also provided on this excursion. With drinks in hand and the sun beaming from above, it was time to set the mood with the lyrical styling of none other than Shaggy. Our peaceful serene boat ride had turned into a rocking dance party cruise, and we were not the slightest bit mad about it. Everyone was having a great time.

After a few minutes' ride across the waterway, we approached the famed landmark Rick's Café, known to travelers worldwide for incredible sunsets and epic cliff div-ing that occurs from the ledges surrounding the café. Cliff jumping in Negril was not something on my bucket list, but Leiselle and I thought, *We are here, so, sure why not!* I'm cer-tain that now I understand the phrase liquid courage. As we approached the cliff with our entourage of party boat dance partners, I grew more and more excited at the opportunity to plummet into the waters below.

But the same excitement that roared from my body was quickly replaced with an overwhelming sense of anxiety as I approached the ledge and peered down to the glassy waters below.

"Should I really be able to see the bottom," I asked; the words *spinal cord injury* would not leave the forefront of my thoughts.

There were lines of people all around ready to jump… and every few moments, the number of people standing and stalling my inevitable demise decreased. After a few jumpers splashed down below, I found myself standing on the precipice looking down.

"How do I do it?" I asked with the inconsistent vocalizations of a woman certain of her death. The cliff attendant said, "Just put your feet over the edge, then we will count three… two… one, then you jump." Seemed so simple. With the crowd of onlookers cheering from behind, I stepped to the edge and awaited the attendant's voice.

Three…

Two…

One…

Jump!

At that moment, I learned to fly.

An absolute rush of adrenaline surged through my body. My arms stretched out from my body as if I was capturing the wind within my reach. I felt electrified and invigorated as my toes cut through the water below as if to carve out my landing! I felt the splash encapsulate me in a sense of accomplishment and propel me back to the surface with an acknowledgment of my survival.

It was such a triumphant experience… So, I did it again, and so did Leiselle!

It's funny, as a kid, some of the first games we learn to play involve jumping. We find so much joy in these activities. Hopscotch. Jump rope. Leapfrog. But as we grow up, we tend to keep our feet firmly planted on the ground. We find that sometimes, the only thing separating what we are from what we want to be is our own willingness to jump and take the leap.

Not everything is going to line up precisely the way we wish. There will be gaps and valleys, uncertainty and fear. There will be a clash of energies, both pulling you back and urging you to jump at the same time. But in the end, it all comes down to your willingness to open yourself up to the possibilities that exist. It might not always be how you planned, but it will change your life, and you will never have to regret not making a move.

So, think about where you want to be, take a deep breath, count yourself down: Three… two… one… JUMP!

You just might find that when you land, you have a few more things to be thankful for!

After returning from Jamaica with a new appreciation for what the holidays could be, I was ready to welcome in more of a traditional holiday experience. With Thanksgiving in the books and Christmas just around the corner, the holiday spirit was intensifying. After my experience on those cliffs and much-needed time away from my typical day-to-day, I felt a little more open to the charm of it all. I started to embrace some of the nostalgia that I initially wanted to escape. It wasn't easy at first—the holidays bring with them the inevitable reminders of how things used to be—but I was hopeful that there could still be joy in what was left. After all, I really do love the holidays.

You know what else I love? Canada. It had been a few weeks since I left the Caribbean, and my tan was starting to fade. It seemed like the perfect timing to trade in my brightly colored swimsuit for the cozy comfort of my favorite winter scarf. With Christmas just a few days away, I was looking forward to experiencing the wintery wonderland that is Montreal in December. Who better to do this with than my childhood friend and soon to be travel adventure partner, Jennifer.

Jennifer was always up for an adventure and was at a place in her life where being spontaneous could work. I always had a lot of fun spending time with her and never had to worry about acting a certain way. I could always be my ridiculous, crazy, uninhibited self around her. That is the joy of having a friend that has literally seen you at your best, worst, and everywhere in between. Jennifer and I decided we would do it up for a weekend in Montreal under the agreement that we would embrace the holidays in whatever way we wanted to in the moment.

One of my favorite things about Christmas growing up was getting together with the family to decorate the tree. This was another tradition for my family. My dad would typically go out and find the biggest tree on the lot. Then he would enlist my brothers to cut off about three feet of it, then get it home only to realize it wouldn't fit in the house. After the ceiling had just the right amount of tree scratches, we would pull out all of the ornament boxes and go to town. Most of my time was spent placing and then removing my ornaments after being told, "That doesn't go there, Dev."

After finishing decorating, typically, some catastrophic event would happen that required reapplication of several decorations. Usually, this was attributed to the excitement of the dog, the curiosity of the grandkids, or the not-so-uncommon living room wrestling matches between my brothers. Regardless, decorating (and redecorating) the tree was always a lot of fun. So, one of the first things Jennifer and I decided to do was embrace our own version of this tradition.

After arrival and settling into our hotel room, we made the decision that we were going to start the holiday off strong with a quest to find the perfect Christmas tree. Mind you, when we say "perfect tree," that meant one with decorations that could sit on the nightstand of our hotel room, one we probably wouldn't be heartbroken over when we threw it out after our trip. We made our way to the local shopping mall. Montreal's weather is known for a little bit of unpredictability at times. Because of this, Montreal has essentially built a city under the city to provide some shelter from the elements. People can head beneath the streets to find a plethora of winding corridors filled with shops, restaurants, and the occasional gelato stand!

As we made our way around this elaborate hallway labyrinth-equivalent of a cornstalk maze in the fall, we stumbled upon a discount general shop. It was there that it happened. Jennifer and I met the absolute love of our lives. Okay, maybe just the love of our weekend. The tallest of his peers, so handsomely dressed in the deepest shade of green that boldly contrasted the white walled shelves behind him. No matter what directional view you took, his body was captivating. Without hesitation, Jennifer and I knew we had to have him. We emerged from the store with our newfound two-foot-tall love: Trevor the tree. We named him Trevor because it just seemed like a fitting name for a tree.

In addition to Trevor, we also picked up a few other items along our way: some miniature ornaments to adorn him, some festive holiday hats, and of course, a bottle of red wine.

After finishing our shopping, we emerged from the underground, and the three of us—Jennifer, Trevor, and I—made our way back to the hotel.

Later that evening, Jennifer and I took in some of the city sights as we walked through the streets of downtown Montreal and headed to dinner. We enjoyed a lovely meal complete with a few beer flights. What better way to experience a new city than to sample some of their local brews? Little did we know, the beer tasting would actually go on to become a daily activity.

After dinner, we frolicked our way back to the hotel and threw our very own Christmas party, complete with music, laughter, and good cheer. We donned our stylish Christmas hats, poured our wine into our paper cups, and trimmed our tree. Trevor never looked better, and we loved it! Thus, the theme of our weekend emerged, "J'adore Trevor," said with the most inauthentic drawn-out attempt at a French accent. You know, because we loved our new tree and because we wanted to speak a little French of our own since everyone else in the region seemed to be bilingual.

My apologies to the people of Montreal that may have heard this phrase echoing throughout the streets over the course of that week. It just brought us so much joy as it rolled off the tongue.

The rest of the weekend was filled with even more joy and laughter. We went ice skating at the riverfront, made snow angels in the park, wrapped a scarf around the snowman we built, sang Christmas carols, roasted marshmallows in the Christmas village, and we even took a picture with none other than Santa himself.

We laughed to the point of tears. We embraced the holiday spirit. We made shadow puppets on the wall. We sang at the top of our lungs. We took a Nordic plunge into freezing cold water, followed by a refreshing nap in the nap rooms of the Bota Bota spa. We drank beer—a lot of beer. And we watched the most spectacular fireworks display over the water set to a soundtrack of holiday favorites. It wasn't about fancy restaurants, extravagant items, or adrenaline-rushing adventures; instead, it was about simple pleasures. That weekend taught me to embrace all moments and those that we share them with. I found that at times when the light seems a little dim, you just need to step back and find joy in the little things and comfort in the company.

J'adore Trevor!

CHAPTER 5

WONDERS OF THE WORLD

———

"The moment you take responsibility for everything in your life is the moment you can change anything in your life"

—HAL ELROD

Have you ever just been struck by a random inner impulse of spontaneity? Maybe you woke up one day and just decided to play hooky from work. Or maybe you've purchased something just because you wanted to, without much thought or research behind the purchase? I do not consider myself spontaneous in the slightest, but there is something to be said for the occasional desire to throw caution to the wind and see where it takes you. It is a different kind of adrenaline rush when you begin to take responsibility for your life in an instant and make choices that you might not have been inclined to make before.

Later on, as I sat nestled into the crook of my couch waiting for the sun to rise outside of my living room window, I found myself thinking about all of the places I'd been and the things I'd done in just over six months. I felt like I was truly starting to understand the essence of Mr. Elrod's statement. It was as though I would barely recognize that disappointed woman that stumbled across her empty passport, holding in it the weight of a thousand excuses. It was that moment that forced me to take responsibility for my story—and what a difference doing so made!

Do you remember those "choose your own ending" books you'd read as a child? The ones that gave you the freedom and the power to write and rewrite your story at any point along the way. They were great, right? As I continued through this wandering adventure, I developed a new appreciation for this ability to craft my own story. To take charge of where I go next. It is a pretty cool experience, to be honest. I would never have imagined the way this story would unfold. I thought back to my first trip of the new year and how it came to be.

I had just finished up a pretty intense semester at the university that created a significant demand on my time. Work had been more chaotic than usual, and honestly, the last few days were a bit taxing. I had also just found out that a patient that I had worked with for quite a while had passed away while I was off. To compound the situation further, the holidays had just passed, and it was going to be my birthday, a day I typically dread because it only reminds me that I am another year older and yet still no closer to where I thought I would be.

Between the sheer degree of exhaustion and the emotional drain I had been feeling, I was burnt out and needed a break from life. I was feeling defeated, and my sense of self-worth was dwindling. I couldn't just sit at home and wallow in doubt and self-pity. I was yearning for a little salty air and calm ocean breeze. My colleague/friend had also just survived a similar series of life events, and she, too, was ready for a little change in scenery. So just like that, we got on the internet and booked our trip to Playa del Carmen, Mexico. Talk about spontaneous.

Upon arrival at our resort, a sense of pure calm and relaxation resonated around us. The welcome drinks at check-in seemed to taste ever-so-sweet. Fresh chilled fruit mingled with my lips as the glass tipped a little more than slightly as if to pour paradise directly into my soul. The smell of the ocean provided a clean cut to the aroma of coconut that lingered through the air. I'm still not sure if that scent was the fresh coconuts being cut from the trees or if it was the manufactured chemicals that made up the various sunscreens slathered on every human we encountered. To be honest, it didn't matter because it was a constant reminder that I was not in Kansas anymore. (Truth be told, I've never been to Kansas.)

We walked down a winding pathway lined with the most vibrant tropical flowers. The breeze blew across the leaves of the towering palm trees, creating a gentle shushing sound as if it to tell our bodies to relax. When we arrived at our room, there was a lengthy white birthday banner adorning the door. I reached for the handle, and with a swipe of my access card, a little green light appeared—granting us access into our new temporary home. As I opened the door, my gaze was immediately attracted to the plethora of rainbow-colored balloons spread out across the beds. What an adorable little gesture.

As I scanned the room to take it all in, I noticed the luxurious Turkish robes waiting in the closet and an abundantly stocked bar with a plethora of local liquors. Now, I'm not typically a big hard liquor person, but let's just say I let the spirits move me (see what I did there). As we began to unpack and settle in, it was as though all reservations and tension just melted away, and a little bit of delirium set in (in the most fun way). We found ourselves right in the middle of a mental state that I like to refer to as the "super sillies." This is when adults run and jump on beds, dance around the room, laugh to the point of tears as if shedding the inhibitions of adulthood and just relishing in the pure joy of the present moment. It was awesome!

As our week progressed, we threw caution to the wind and just went with the carefree flow of things. There were aqua aerobics, tacos, shows, yoga, poolside naps, great conversation, and we even got to drive speedboats through the mangroves while making our way to visit the fishies. How many people get the chance to just throw their hands up and fly across the crystal blue waters at maximum speed without a care in the world? It was so refreshing, energizing, and exactly what we needed.

In recalling the events of that trip, I can't help but think about one of our morning excursions that prompted me to see things from a different perspective.

I was sitting on what I could only describe as a questionably functioning small tour bus with twelve other individuals with whom I was sure to become acquainted over the course of the next few hours. We had been listening to the most eclectic mix of music. The type of not-so-common playlist that starts with the Rocky theme song "Eye of the Tiger" before easing ever-so-abruptly into a little Michael Jackson montage. The surprises kept coming, with a transition that connected Michael Bolton to The Beach Boys. Tie in a little Latin vibe, and you were right there with us. I did say eclectic.

We were driving alongside the Mexican jungle, various

shades of greenery lining the road and creating a lush canopy as far as the eyes could see. My new travel companions and I were making our way through time, heading back to the ancient world to explore the incredible ruins of what has been named one of the new Wonders of the World: Chichen Itza in the Yucatan Peninsula, Mexico.

The crazy thing about this particular sunrise trek was that just a few short days before, I had no idea what I would be doing on that day. And then, without research or a plan, I found myself enjoying a beautiful sunrise from the perch of my notably worn-down leather bench seat in that rattling metal box on wheels. As I bobbed up and down with each pothole, headed on another once-in-a-lifetime adventure, I could not help but feel a sense of elation from my last-minute plan.

I also felt slightly carsick.

I can't help but chuckle to myself when I think about how I got there. I think about how quickly that adventure came to fruition at a time when I absolutely needed it most. One minute I was sitting at home, wondering if I was going to miss out on a month of travel, and the next thing you know, I was puddling along on this bus ride, trying to avoid too many collisions between my head and the window with each jarring bump.

The entire experience came together beautifully despite not having planned it in advance. The resort, the food, the excursions—it was an incredible trip. I can't help but wonder, how on earth did those opportunities present themselves in what seemed to be such perfect timing? Then I remembered that the opportunities were the result of my own choices.

There are a lot of times in life when we wake up wondering who we are, where we are, and how on earth did we get here? Well, the answer to that is a simple one. We are exactly who we allow ourselves to be and where we allow our life to take us. Yes, life has a way of throwing things at us—things that can be cruel and unusual at times, things that can break us down. What we must realize is that we are not defined by our circumstances. We are defined by the responses to those circumstances. Let's face it, about the only thing we truly can control in the chaos is our response. So, who we are, where we end up, and how we got there are all the result of the choices we make in response to life.

So today, choose yourself. Choose your life. Choose your adventure. Choose where you want to go and how you're going to get there. Choose love. Choose joy. Choose how much sugar you put in your coffee.

Choose to live the life that makes you excited for what the day will bring, whether it's waking up with an adventure on the agenda or just spending time with good company. And while you are making those choices, think about why.

Do you need a little break from life, a chance to recuperate?

Do you just need the comfort of a friend who can let you feel all the feels?

Do you need an afternoon of pampering or a really nice night out on the town?

Regardless of what you think your reasons are, remember the ultimate reason should always be the same: because You Are Worth IT!

Don't let life keep you down. Instead let it build you up. Let your choices today be the foundation to the pyramid that is your life! And when life gets tough, remember those adventure books. If you didn't like the path you were on, you could just turn the page and make a different choice.

Today, write your own adventure and make your life worthy of the greatness you deserve!

Be your own Wonder of the World!

CHAPTER 6

TRAINS, PLANES, AND DOGSLEDS

I was sitting in our Helsinki hotel room, peering through the windows while the snow made its attempt to impede us yet again. Typically, fresh falling snow would have quite the calming effect, but after the events preceding our arrival, I couldn't help but feel a bit anxious as I watched the airy white flakes dance through the night's sky.

Let me set the stage a little bit more…

First European adventure scheduled. I had been counting down to this once-in-a-lifetime vacation for over six months. To top it off, I was going to spend this trip hanging out with my incredible sister, Donna, who I missed very much. We lived about 450 miles away from each other and hadn't seen each other in a while.

We had been having constant group messages about the trip for several weeks. These messages had been quite comical because we kept mixing up dates and times etc. My niece, Lauren, would say, "You guys are going to be great traveling."

I detected a bit of sarcasm. Perhaps this was warranted. Let me explain…

Vacation Day, February 2018, 2:35 a.m.

Airline alert sounds on my phone. "Flight to Boston canceled due to weather."

Seriously?

As I rubbed the blurred bits of sleep from my eyes, I scrolled through the airline notifications on my phone to try and figure things out. I started by getting the phone number for customer service at the airline and called to speak to a representative. Fortunately, I had learned to expect the unexpected when it comes to travel, so I made sure that there was a little wiggle room in the travel plan, approximately thirty-six hours before heading off to Europe. With a blizzard striking the northeast, thirty-six hours did not bring with it the amount of comfort I had initially hoped. The main goal: get to Boston in time to catch a 10 p.m. flight to Finland the next day (just remember that—10 p.m. flight).

So, after an hour of calls, text messages, and app updates, I had been booked and rebooked on a total of five different trips to various airports in and around Boston and Rhode Island. I figured if I got close enough, I could figure out a way to get there. So, the final verdict was to change my 3 p.m. flight out of North Carolina to a flight that was now leaving at 5:40 a.m. Good thing I packed the night before! Knowing I only had about two hours to get ready and be at the gate, I jumped out of bed, showered, fed the dog, made the bed, and left for the airport.

My connection put me in Philadelphia by 7:30 a.m., where my sister Donna picked me up. Since all flights from Philadelphia to Boston were impacted by the snow, we opted to travel up by train. I was midair when my sister booked the train tickets, so it was a welcome and pleasant surprise to find we were booked for first class. Thanks, Donna! This was a nice treat. Mimosas, charcuterie tray, internet, phone service, a full dining table, and plenty of room to nap. My niece, Lauren, who lives in Boston, offered to pick us up from the train station when we arrived. Poor kid, we kept telling her the wrong station, so she spent the better part of the morning driving around the city. No wonder she had a little sarcasm to her. After a few adjustments, we finally were on the same page, and she arrived to pick us up. In exchange for our ridiculousness, I offered to treat her to lunch.

We enjoyed a delicious lunch filled with great conversation, then spent some time meandering around the city. Given my body's need to adjust from the early morning excitement, I was pretty exhausted by the time the evening came to an end and welcomed a good night's rest. The next morning, I woke up and checked us in for our flight that evening. My sister and I spent the day lounging around, catching up, playing with cameras, and getting excited. We were also starting to grow a bit anxious as the forecast started to shift, and the heaviest portion of snow was now predicted to start falling an hour before our flight. Ha or so I thought.

Apparently, I had been misreading the reservation for over six months (thanks military time), and our flight was actually set to leave two hours earlier, not 10 p.m. like I had previously thought! Great news from the weather perspective, but man, if this was any indication of how the traveling was going to go, we would need to alter the over/under on whether or not we would survive.

Regardless, this made for some incredible memories, provided a lot of laughter, and really just reinforced how much fun it could be to just enjoy the ride.

That evening, we arrived at the Boston terminal and were able to board our flight rather quickly. We settled into our seats, ordered our meals, and celebrated with the first of many toasts while the plane took to the skies headed to our first connection in Iceland.

The flight itself was not too bad (thanks to a little first-class upgrade). I took full advantage of the extra space and closed my eyes for a short preparatory nap. Before I knew it, I was waking up just in time to watch the descent over the Scandinavian Mountain range. Once we made landfall, my sister and I headed to the lounge. The lounge in Iceland was packed with delicious coffee, and you guessed it, chocolate! We took full advantage of the pause in our adventure by thoroughly indulging in a little chocolate buffet for breakfast, or dinner, or whatever it was. Time change is no joke. After taking on enough sugar to incite a brief surge and subsequent crash of energy, we rested up and awaited the call for boarding. After a few hours, we were back on the plane and off to Helsinki.

The first task after landing in Helsinki was to retrieve our luggage and make our way to the taxi. Crossing over to the car line was like a real-life version of Frogger (the nineteen-eighties video game that has a frog dodging traffic with futile attempts to reach the other side). Luckily for us, we made it across the traffic lanes no worse for wear. A short car ride later, we arrived in the downtown harbor area of Helsinki. Now, this was a pretty cool little gem of a city. There were beautiful churches, cute little coffee shops, and even a small version of the Parisian Love Lock Bridge. My sister and I spent the afternoon taking a little stroll around the harbor town. We enjoyed the breathtaking scenery, from beautiful Neoclassical architecture to the notable Nordic elements that are ingrained into almost every establishment, including the large ships in the harbor that seem kin to those of fabled pirates.

We decided we had to be those tourists who pay an exuberant amount of money for a five-minute ride on the Ferris wheel, because, why not? What we did not realize was that this little attraction would give us a glimpse into the true naked spirit of Helsinki, literally!

Right beneath the Ferris wheel was an outdoor swimming pool, that's right, outdoors! Now, this might be great on an eighty-degree summer day, but we were in Finland in March, and the temperature outside was twenty-eight degrees. Typically, when the weather is twenty-eight degrees in the middle of winter, our pools back home are covered over and closed; however, in Finland there was nothing covered up, like literally nothing. The swimmers in the pool had no clothes on! I mean if you squinted really close you might have seen the outline of a thong speedo, but for the most part, we are talking frozen flesh. It was in that discovery that I realized my year of "yes" to adventures may actually require some lines to be drawn. The idea of hypothermia seemed a little too adventurous for this girl, but like I said, the scenery was breathtaking.

After a little more exploration and laughter, we made our way back to the hotel to settle in for the night. We had an early flight the next morning to Lapland, although the bare-skinned visions of the day had me slightly rethinking our next accommodation—an igloo in the arctic circle. *Maybe I should have packed more thermal socks!* And just as that thought crossed my mind, the snow started falling once again as if to draw a curtain close on this installment of trains, planes, and automobiles.

As I watched the flakes slowly descend through the frame of the window, I had a slight moment of panic, thinking "not again," but just as quickly as the thought entered, I remembered how everything had actually worked out pretty well despite the chaos. I chose to accept fate and drifted off to sleep.

As the sun came up over Helsinki, it revealed freshly fallen snow in a beautiful blanket over the city. However, the most calming view was that of the dark black pavement that made up the freshly plowed, unimpeded streets. Turns out, when snow is in the daily forecast, you get pretty good at snow removal. This was an incredibly welcome sight as it meant that our path to the airport, and more so to our next Finnish location, was clear.

After a short one-hour flight, we found ourselves situated in the heart of Finnish Lapland at the breathtaking Kakslauttanen Arctic Resort. Kakslauttanen is a vast wilderness area located right off the highway to the Arctic Sea. The region has been home to the Sami for over a century. From the moment we arrived, we felt immersed in the welcoming culture and hospitality of the Sami people. Despite the below-freezing temperatures, there was a sense of warmth that encapsulated the area. Our initial draw to the region was to seek out a glimpse of the aurora borealis (also known as the Northern Lights), but we were looking forward to learning more about the culture and the land during our stay.

Once we arrived at the resort, the hospitality continued as we were escorted to our igloo. Now, when I say igloo, let me give you a true depiction of our accommodations. Imagine a five-star cottage with its own sauna, gorgeous authentic decor of deer hides, and furniture made of wooden timbers that look like they had just been cut down from the forest outside. There was a large living room with a beautiful cast-iron log fireplace sitting as a focal point in the corner and a full-sized kitchen area equipped with all of the modern conveniences. In all, it had an exorbitant amount of space but felt as cozy as ever. Attached to the large cottage space were the igloo-shaped bedrooms made of Kelo glass, allowing an almost 360° view of the open wilderness and beautiful starry night sky.

After spending the day exploring the snow-covered resort, my sister and I settled in for our first night's sleep in the "igloo." Typically, most people would not be very happy when they're woken up in the middle of the night by blaring sirens, especially one that's as loud as fire alarm. The kind that puts your body into an instant state of elevated heart rate and panic. Surprisingly, we were not "most people." In fact, my sister and I could barely sleep due to the overwhelming anticipation of the alarm sounding. We laid there in our little beds, staring up through the glass ceiling of our igloo, looking at the backdrop of the dark evening sky. The edges of the frame were illuminated by the glow of freshly fallen snow. The sky was so clear and the stars so big, you felt like you could just reach out and grab them. There was only one thing we didn't see looking up. As we laid there and the night crept upon us, the anticipation continued to build—much like it does for a child in bed, straining their ears to listen for sleigh bells on Christmas Eve.

Interestingly, there was an internal battle beginning to incite in me, one that posed the excitement of possibility against the sheer exhaustion that was consuming my body after three days of travel. Just as it appeared the fatigue was about to deliver the knockout blow, the bell sounded… and by bell I mean the glorious, instantly energizing sound of the infamous *aurora alarm*.

As the alarm began blaring and piercing through the night's calm, my sister and I sprang up from our respective beds and staggered our way across to the doorway to the front closet where our winter boots were lying in wait. We got on our snow pants and boots quicker than a fireman suiting up for a five-alarm fire, then bolted out the door with the same hurry. Apparently, we were not the only ones excited by this event, as almost every other guest in the Lapland resort had rushed out into the bitter cold as if we were starting an arctic flash mob. Cameras in hand, settings adjusted, and our eyes peering to the darkness—all just in time. At that moment, the skies lit up with an effervescent shade of green as the celestial winds danced across the skyline. Alas, the torment turned into reward on our first night as my sister, and I bore witness to the incredible phenomenon known as the Northern Lights.

Rumor has it that just because you spend an exorbitant amount of money and head to the Arctic Circle, there is no guarantee that those pesky lights will make an appearance and dance synchronously through your visual fields. But that didn't stop us from chasing after them every night. During the days, we filled our time exploring the vast wilderness that makes up the Finnish winter wonderland. We went on walks around the resort, stopped for photo ops, and each day brought with it a once-in-a-lifetime adventure that we might not have necessarily been exposed to anywhere else.

As we walked around the resort, you could hear the breeze become silent, almost giving way to the sound of falling snow. It was easy to be present in the moment and find the beauty in the sounds of the crunch beneath our feet and the inhalation and sound of each breath. Occasionally, we did encounter the lively "beast" that inhabits the land. As he first approached, we couldn't help but take notice of his mammoth size and blinding white hair that almost blended into the surroundings. He moved gracefully through the landscape with a slow, methodical stride. As the beast drew closer, you could hear the most subtle jingle sound muted against his body. As he came near, his cadence slowed ever so slightly. And just when the beast would come within arm's reach, you could make out a glisten in his eyes.

He was the sweetest 160 pound Malamute dog that strolled the land at his leisure.

Speaking of dogs, our first major adventure on the docket was a Donna and Devon attempt at dog sledding. This was a good one!

As we arrived at the excursion, we were given a brief introduction into what the dog sledding adventure would entail, and we learned a little bit about the history of how dog sleds and dog teams are put together and used throughout the Arctic. After the introduction, we were taken out to meet our team of canines that would inevitably give us the grand tour of the Arctic. Once we met our team, we were provided with instructions on how to operate the sled, control the steering, and ultimately how to use the brakes. This last piece of education came in handy because dog sleds go a lot faster than one might anticipate.

The energetic dogs stood at the ready, and with a strong call of "mush," the team made their way across the land, over the hills, and around the bend of this great wintry wilderness. Steering a dog sled is *not* easy. It takes quite a lot of effort, and you're doing so with the amount of adrenaline you might expect for someone that just had three shots of epinephrine squeezed into them. As difficult as it was, what a great experience. The halfway point of our trek was in a notably large clearing in the forest. This wide-open space was the perfect backdrop for a scenic photo op with our team of canine companions. After the guide took a few snaps for us with our phones, we prepared to make the turn to head back through the route that we came.

My sister and I decided to switch positions at this point so that she could also experience the thrill of driving the sled, and I could capture some really great footage for a memory video. Throughout my travels, I'd tried to document with video memories and blogs to capture the experience, the joys, and the excitement through each of those crazy adventures. As I secured myself within the sled, I loaded up the camera on video mode and positioned myself in a way where I was ready to take on some great B-roll footage. What I did not anticipate was that this video shoot would ultimately become more appropriate for a bloopers reel.

As we started to head down the hill and pick up speed, the dogs were in the rhythm and rushing through the snow at a rapid pace. This is not typically an issue for the straight-aways; however, we were about to encounter something not-so-straight. As we came down the hill, we started a series of turns that one might equate to the drastic switchbacks of an Olympic bobsled track. With each turn navigation, my sister steered the sled brilliantly—with one exception. Just as we were coming around what almost appeared to be a hard 90° turn, I began to sense our speed was picking up a little bit more. I thought to myself, *Go Donna, she is racing this thing like a champ.* Each turn kept getting a little bit more intense, and our speed continued to grow.

I started giving some soft verbal cues to initiate a little bit more use of the brake, you know, so I could maintain the footage (definitely not because I was scared).

However, verbal cues against the sound of mushing and dogs speeding through crunchy snowy terrain are easily drowned out.

But ALAS! Speed would no longer be an issue as we came to a screeching halt by way of an overturned sled, launching me into the comfort and embrace of the ice-cold snow.

At this point, I sat up, brushed myself off, and couldn't help but laugh as my sister started chasing the dogs and sled that had taken off on its course back home without us.

Looking back on that moment has given me one of the most hilarious turn of events I can remember. I'm pretty sure my sister and I both experienced a slight bit of incontinence, not only at the point of impact but also with each bit of laughter that occurred every time we have retold our story since. Mind you, I don't believe that it was intentional on Donna's part—driving a dog's sled is "ruff," but that's not to say that I probably haven't given my sister plenty of reason to want to flip me out of a sled over the course of my lifetime.

After we did finally make it back to camp with our entire team somewhat intact, we sat to enjoy a lovely post-trek tradition: a hot ladle of fresh soup, warm bread, music, storytelling, and fireside conversation in a reindeer hide teepee. After we warmed up a bit, we made our way over to meet the pups-in-training. We got to play with the newest additions to the canine family. I mean, who doesn't love playing with puppies? Puppies make everything better.

After our incredible adventure across the northern lands, we made it back to our igloo, only mildly worse for wear. After a steaming hot shower, I settled myself under the most comfortable fluffy down comforter and enjoyed the ambient warmth of the crackling fireplace. As I laid in bed, I found myself anxiously awaiting the wake-up call from the aurora alarm once again.

There are many moments in our lives that don't always go according to plan, no matter how much we think we are prepared. We must be willing to adapt to the unpredictability that comes in moments that are beyond our control. Moral of the story, sometimes life throws you curves, and the best thing you can do is roll with it, and sometimes those curves will give you no choice but to roll—through snow, like you have been launched out of a speeding sled.

CHAPTER 7

HANGING BY A THREAD

Have you ever decided to do something so crazy that the people around you might question your sanity? Something so ridiculous that there is a brief moment where you begin to question it as well? The cascading waters rushed over me as I dangled with nothing but rough strands of twine interlaced together holding me in suspension high above the earth's surface. In that moment, I couldn't help but wonder... what was I thinking?

I remember sitting down at my kitchen table with the glow of the computer screen reflecting at me. The steam of my coffee was rising into the atmosphere with a comforting aroma that I have come to crave. The computer screen was emitting a systematic influx of enticing images with each click. I glanced through each as I tried to figure out how to fill in the gaps of what I had by then deemed my year of yes. As I was searching through, the mysterious force that conditions the internet kicked in and predicted the future. An advertisement came across for waterfall rappelling in the rain forest. *Eureka, that's it!* Work had been a bit stressful, and finals were coming up at the university, so I was feeling like I was reaching my limits.

What do you do when you feel like you're at the end of your rope?

Simple: tie the rope to a rock and rappel down a waterfall.

In that very moment, I knew this would be my next adventure. I internally asked myself, *Should this be a solo trip, or do I invite a friend?* I pondered the thought for several moments and wondered who would be crazy enough to entertain the idea of hanging off a jagged cliff, under rushing water, suspended above river, with nothing more than a half-inch thick piece of string… well that's easy—Jennifer!

One of the best things about Jennifer is she's one of those friends that you can call with nearly no advance notice and say, "hey do you want to go on an adventure" and almost certainly, her answer is yes. I'm very fortunate to have a friend like her in my life. She embraces the spontaneity and helps fuel my curiosity for this incredible world. So, Jennifer and I booked our flights, signed up for our waterfall extravaganza, and waited patiently for a long weekend trip to arrive.

When we landed in Puerto Rico, we made our way to the rental car counter and waited to obtain our keys. Once those were in hand, we loaded the car and set out for our hotel across the island. The weather was rainy and grim, but we did not let the gray skies deflate our enthusiasm. We were on vacation, after all!

However, in booking this trip, I nearly lost sight of the fact that Puerto Rico had been devastated by an unyielding hurricane the year prior. I had not given much thought to the state of the island or how much of an impact would still be noticeable.

We were starkly reminded as we made our way to the resort. Downed trees lined the roadways. Once beautiful, flourishing resorts more closely resembled those abandoned hotels often depicted in horror films, and various wildlife could be seen scrounging for morsels of nourishment on deserted beaches. It was humbling, to say the least.

After spending the night enjoying the resort pool and making friends with some of the local iguanas, Jennifer and I were ready for some excitement. We had plans to embark on our journey into the vast El Yunque rainforest. According to *Discover Puerto Rico*, El Yunque is the only tropical rainforest in the US National Forest Service, and one of Puerto Rico's most beloved natural gems. To say we were stoked would be an understatement.

Our adventure started out a little sketchy. We were advised by the tour company that we would be picked up by tour guides at a predetermined location. Turns out, this location was in a random drugstore parking lot two turns off the highway. As we reached the designated rendezvous point, Jennifer and I couldn't help but be a little taken aback by the run-down appearance. Crumbled pavement riddled with potholes, stagnant puddles of water emitting the odor of old gym socks left out in ninety-degree heat, and storefronts with cracked windows and torn signage. The whole scene was a little unnerving. As the van pulled up, we scurried on board, delighted to escape our surroundings. We headed into the rainforest for a day of zip-lining, hiking, and waterfall rappelling with Rocaliza Adventure Tours.

Once we arrived on site, we deboarded our transport van and made our way over to be fit for our equipment. Jennifer and I donned our protective gear then convened with the group for a short trek into the wild to meet the river.

During our walk, the guide pointed out the stunted height and scarce, thin greenery of the existing vegetation in the region, and told stories of the impact the forceful wind and rain had on the land. The towering umbrella of trees once graciously provided shelter and security for the smaller foliage below. All that was wiped out in an instant, thrusting the seedlings below into maturation way before their time. The way this story seemed to parallel life itself in so many ways was not lost on me.

We made our way to the water's edge, secured our packs, and did one last check of our safety gear before wading into the chilly river stream. In lockstep with our guide, we scrambled up the river and climbed across rocks as we navigated through luscious greenery during our ascent to the top. Along the climb, we stopped at several incredible locations for photoshoots and action videos. There was one photo spot where large rocks in the center of the path created the most surreal platform—a stage if you will—with an opportunistic backdrop full of natural elements that would make a landscape painter jealous. Then there were spots where our guides curated the most riveting action-adventure shots. You could tell they had done this a time or two, and it was apparent that our guides were well-seasoned in the art of the experience. All for "the gram" as they said.

As we broached the precipice, we were greeted by the thunderous sound of rushing water making its way through the rock line and plummeting into the canyon below. It was my sincere hope that it would only be the water plummeting and not my body. As we came to the edge, our guides rounded us up for one last lesson on the ropes and belaying system. We gave confirmation of our understanding, then one by one, we made our way to the platform for the adrenaline rush ahead.

Jennifer preceded me on the platform. As she secured her harness to the line, I stepped into the role of videographer set to document the awesomeness that was to come (at least that was what I was hoping for). And in true Jennifer fashion, she tamed that wild waterfall with ease!

I stepped to the edge, ready to do the same.

As I inched my way forward ever so slightly, I could feel the earth trembling around me. I grasped the strands of nylon rope between my hands with a bone-crushing grip and altered my position around the rock's edge. I embraced the platform beneath my feet as my senses elevated into a distinct awareness of existence.

As my guide instructed, I widened my stance and leaned back into the cavernous void dangling from the rock-face like a marionette puppet.

My knees were trembling as I started to initiate my descent.

And with that first push, I felt this sense of energy rush over me as the flowing waters gushed across my body. Powerful enough to cut a forceful path through the stone and rapid as a raging sea. My guide shouted out to me:

"Do not fight the water. Embrace it!"

What a powerful perspective. I couldn't help but linger on this thought, and what an inspiring mentality from someone who I was sure had witnessed the devastation of waters beyond his control! With each bounce from the rock, the muscles in my cheeks stretched more and more until reaching a point at which a permanent grin stretched from ear to ear. I felt the force of nature crashing upon me with the continuous weight of gravity as I made my descent through the roaring waters—but instead of the weight crushing me, it lifted me in a way I could have never imagined. I peered upward in awe with an inexplicable degree of appreciation.

Standing at the bottom, I could not help but reflect upon the motivational instructions provided at the top. The forces of nature can be funny sometimes, occasionally the waters can rage in ways that devastate us and knock down the strongest and tallest among us, but the water can also invigorate and renew us.

Sometimes in life, we have no control over the impact the water will have, sometimes the water will generate fears and anxiety far beyond our comprehension, but sometimes the water can calm us, center us, and put us in a position to withstand the force it thrusts upon us if we are willing to go with it. And sometimes, if we're really lucky, the water strengthens us.

CHAPTER 8

HIGHWAY TO HEAVEN

———

"There are places on earth where we can catch a glimpse of heaven."

—ANTHONY DOUGLASS WILLIAMS

I know everyone at some point in their life has gone on some sort of road trip. Many might say it is a rite of passage. Driving down the open road with the lyrical styling of your favorite eighties rock band reverberating through the speakers. The car filled with the best selection of snacks, from donut holes to beef jerky, and all that lies ahead is the open road. It's usually scenic in nature, and at some point, it is inevitable that something memorable will happen along the way. After all, a good road trip is less about the destination and more about the journey, right? The only three rules of the road:

Rule 1: keep the jams coming
Rule 2: pay attention to the signs
Rule 3: surround yourself with good company

Fortunately for me, this road trip checked all three boxes and then some.

Planned with a lot of forethought, I set out on a flight to Las Vegas, Nevada, to meet up with two other easy-going individuals: my really good friend, Patricia, and the other a perfect stranger who would soon become a friend as well. We planned a four-day road trip through the national parks of the southwest that would start in the electrifying city of Las Vegas. After an evening of anticipation, we would then hit the road the next morning, heading out to the great wide open. Our first destination would take us to the Navajo Nation of Page, Arizona, where we would explore the majestic slot canyons referred to as Antelope Canyon. While in Page, we also planned to take advantage of the scenic views overlooking Horseshoe Bend. The next day we would make our way to the giant natural amphitheater of Bryce Canyon and close out our adventure with two days of exploration of some of the most iconic peaks that make up Zion National Park in Springdale, Arizona. It was sure to be an action-packed agenda.

The arrival in Las Vegas went smoothly, which in and of itself is a feat to brag about since we were coordinating three individuals arriving on three different flights from three different airports. Given my history with flight changes and delays, I was elated to find that somehow we managed to plan it so that the timing was perfect. After a short interaction with the car rental attendant, I was given the keys to our SUV and subsequently went on to pick up my traveling companions. We loaded up the luggage, performed our introductions, and then headed off to the hotel.

We stayed at the Luxor Hotel & Casino. This is a unique hotel, notably recognizable due to its thirty story Pyramid that overlooks the Las Vegas Strip. As we walked through the main door, we were thrust into the scene of ancient Egypt. There were towering stone statues of pharaohs set against the backdrop of artistically designed tombs and temple walls adorned with various hieroglyphic symbols. It was quite a bit to take in. As we strolled around the hotel in search of some late evening sustenance, we could not help but chuckle at our choice location for dinner: Diablo's Cantina. Maybe the ancient Egyptians had the same appreciation for tacos that we did. We grabbed a quick bite to eat and settled in for the evening so that we could hit the road early.

When morning came, the three of us were ready to set out with the rising sun. Well, maybe the sun beat us to it, but hey, it's vacation! We made a quick stop off for snacks, coffee, and donut holes before breaking out the playlist and riding off into the grand spaces of the great southwest.

The one thing I learned about road trips early on is I have to pay attention to the signs. The last thing you want to do is miss the signs, both figurative and literal. So, we were intent to make sure that we paid attention to the universe and to every road sign that we came across, including one very unique sign that was quite interesting to see in the middle of a desert. One might expect signs for tumbleweed crossings, mileage, maybe even a sign for food and accommodations, but never once did I expect to come across a sign that said, "Cheese tasting next left!" This was such an intriguing sign to adorn the side of the desert road. So, of course, as good stewards do, we followed the sign!

This sent us down a long winding road with many turns before wrapping around to a little location off the beaten path with a tiny little wood hut, probably no bigger than my walk-in closet. Fresh cheese tasting, I mean, how could we not? We jumped out of the car and danced between the light drops of rain as we and made a path to the door without really knowing what to expect inside. I mean, again, we are in the middle of a desert… not exactly the lush green farmlands where one might expect to see free-range cows roaming.

As we opened the door, we were greeted by an adorable little woman, luminous silver hair spun tightly into a braid and tied back against her scalp, standing behind a refrigerator display filled with, you guessed it, cheese. Every potential cheese you could envision and even some you might not. Armed with toothpicks, we made our way down the curated collection of gourmet cheeses from your basic mild cheddar to "hatch chili," "basil pesto," and a light yet savory special blend named "desert moon" that left our mouths watering for more. My travel companions enjoyed every sampling, including the cheese curds, but I passed on those. Something about the texture of tiny little crumbles that made me a bit hesitant. It was a glorious little pit-stop that somehow sent us on our way with several new additions to the snack supply.

We bid our farewell to the wonderful cheese farm and headed back to the open road. I thought to myself, *If this is in any way an indication of how this trip will go, then this will be quite the delightful adventure.*

I was not wrong. The entire trip was filled with so many wonderful memories and experiences. And the views, my god, the views! No matter where you looked, the landscape was breathtaking. There was something so poetic about the way the sun broke over the ridges and buttes of the mountains. There was an interesting hue of blue that illuminated the sky, providing a stark contrast against the blended mounds of tan and red rock. And, despite the desert climate, there were more trees and greenery than I had envisioned. It was as if the universe set out to paint the most serene work of art with a color palette of infinite shades.

After several hours on the road, we reached Page, Arizona. Coming into the area surrounding Page, we caught a glimpse of Lake Powell. Again, I found myself caught in a trance by the natural juxtaposition where the water meets land. I thought to myself, *Our country has so much more beauty than I have ever been aware of.* It only invigorated my desire to explore more places.

We made the most of our short time in Page, taking on our first short "hike" to the overlook for Horseshoe Bend. This iconic location did not disappoint in the slightest and was quite an easy trek to begin with. My friend, Patricia, served as my personal paparazzi, taking some of my most favorite travel photos. She positioned me mid-frame with the Colorado River wrapping its way around the east rim of the Grand Canyon behind me. While a great occupational therapist, I believe she could surely moonlight as a professional photographer if she so chose.

Come to think of it, Patricia probably could have a plethora of professional endeavors. Perhaps a travel agent? She was the one that planned and organized the whole road trip experience right down to our epic accommodations and all the incredible excursions like the guided tour of Antelope Canyon. In addition to travel agent, she is also a pretty handy mechanic's assistant. Why, might you ask? Well, let me explain.

Driving across the natural landscape of sandy desert, deep canyons, and towering red rocks does not come without risk. Mainly, risk to your rental car security deposit which we became suddenly aware of as we heard a loud smack echo off of the front windshield. At first, it didn't seem to be too concerning, but as we continued to log miles on the road, we realized that maybe we needed to examine the situation a little. Upon inspection, we found that there was a very noticeable dime-size indentation in the glass. While we considered how much more time we planned to spend on the road, I couldn't help but think back on some of my personal history with windshield damage. I knew all too well that that tiny little nick could spider across the span of a windshield in no time. So being three independent women with access to YouTube, we decided to find a local auto store, purchase a repair kit, and take on the work ourselves.

Once we arrived at our next location, Bryce Canyon, we knew we would be spending the duration of the day out exploring. This was the perfect opportunity to apply the repair and let it cure in the sun. Patricia and I educated ourselves via the internet and then went right to work. We methodically followed each step of the instructions, working together synchronously to load the handheld plunger and apply the epoxy with careful consideration not to overfill the edges. Once in place, we applied the curing patch, posed for a picture to document our work, and then set out to explore the sights of Bryce.

After spending the day checking out unique red rock formations, we headed back to our vehicle to check our work. Complete and utter success! It was quite rewarding to see our ingenuity prevail. We closed out our evening we a delicious meal and some live music before heading off to our adorable log cabin to catch some sleep before our next day's adventure to Zion.

Of all the national parks and scenic views we took in over the course of the week, none were more awe-inspiring than those from the peaks of Zion. Truth be told, the trailheads were a bit intimidating but reaching the precipice of those trails was more rewarding than I could have ever imagined. One, in particular, was life changing.

I will forever be changed after reaching the peak of Angel's Landing.

As I reflect on that experience, I can't help but remember the intensity of that climb and how it brought me to life in a way I had never experienced. It was an incredible feeling to have successfully traversed through what seemed like endless switchbacks, ascending elevation gains of 1,500 feet, navigating climbs over pathways no wider than a foot's width at best with nothing but a chain on one side to secure yourself from falling of the ledges of the cliffs.

It was by far the most nerve-racking, gut-wrenching, fear-inducing hike I've ever taken, and with good reason. The feeling, the views, the complete out-of-body experience is something worthy of the protections that nature has created. It felt like the universe was in a constant screening process evidenced by each person that bowed out short of the summit.

As I approached the last phase of this magnificent gauntlet, I became so in tune with each breath, each step… I felt every moment of that incredibly narrow platform, and as I took that last sure-footed step onto the landing, I felt an overwhelming sense of being alive.

I couldn't help but also feel a sense of gratitude to all the encouraging hikers on the trail at 6 a.m. and to my friend Patricia for her willingness to take on that crazy feat with me. But more than anything, I was so indebted with appreciation and respect to the guardians of the universe for providing me with one of the most majestic rewards.

Reaching the peak of Angel's Landing is one of the most profound and defining moments in my life. I can still remember everything about that climb. The enormity of that experience is something that changed me to my core. It was the first time in a very long time that I felt in tune with every fiber of my being and harmonious with the world around me.

I can still remember the way the rocks' unevenness felt beneath my feet, the filling of my lungs as every breath I took resonated through me with each step, the pounding sensation that emerged from my chest and echoed through to my core.

I remember this intense feeling of being alive, 100 percent, truly alive.

It's so easy to get caught up in the chaos around us that we forget what it means to be alive. We constantly take for granted the things that invigorate and give us life under the guise that they will still be there tomorrow.

I write these reflective words after a few years have passed. Now here I am, in the midst of protests for racial injustices and a global pandemic. There is no question, things are horrible right now, and I'm not going to lie, there are moments when I'm watching television or scrolling through social media, and I just feel paralyzed with fear and sadness. But I can't keep doing that.

There needs to be something more.

Maybe this horrible time is an opportunity to reconnect with the things that are important in our lives, the things we often take for granted. Maybe it will help us appreciate those that matter and stop wasting time seeking attention from those that don't. Maybe it will allow the world around us to heal itself from the destruction that we have caused. And maybe, just maybe, it can give us a chance to slow down and breathe.

To be honest, what other choice do we have? It is time to step away from the newscasts that may undoubtedly be setting us up for mental anguish and instead spend more time trying to find ways to celebrate that we are in fact, ALIVE!

CHAPTER 9

AN EPIC JOURNEY

"But you, brave and adept from this day on … there's hope that you will reach your goal … the journey that stirs you now is not far off."

—HOMER

Reading has always been something that has inspired me in my life. Whether it was a simple quote on a candy wrapper, an essay from a famed philosopher, the relatable dialogue of a memoir, or the profound story behind the lines of an epic poem, words have always had a special way of speaking to me and sparking my curiosities far beyond my typical imagination. One story constantly comes to mind and was the inspiration for my next adventure: Homer's *Odyssey*.

If you are not familiar, this is a story told in epic verse that chronicles the twenty-year journey of a man who experiences many trials, tribulations, and hardships over the course of his winding and often indirect route back home to his love after surviving the Trojan War (Homer and Fagles, 1996). I have read this epic poem on several occasions, from high school literature to undergraduate creative humanities courses, and as a self-selected summer reading. I found myself drawn to the style and themes that emerge almost in parallel to the themes of my own life, from hospitality to power struggles, loneliness to loyalty. When thinking about navigating through my own journey of self-discovery during this year of yes, it only seemed fitting to include an exploration of the lands navigated in this epic tale. Plus, I absolutely love Greek mythology!

For the purpose of this adventure, I would need to find my own sea-dwelling vessel that could handle the waters with ease while also providing an appropriate means of shelter, sustenance, and entertainment to get me through dark nautical nights. Ahoy! I believed a cruise ship would suffice! You know who loves cruises? My sister, Donna! The messenger conversation probably went a little something like this.

Me: *Sends a picture of whitewashed buildings with blue domes against a beautiful blue sea*
Me: "Did you get the picture I sent you?"
Donna: "The one of the blue domes? Where is that?"
Me: "It's Santorini, one of the Greek Isles."
Donna: "Oh, very cool. I have a friend that works on a cruise ship out there."
Me: "Nice, if I was going to do a cruise, it would definitely be either an Alaskan cruise or a cruise of the Mediterranean."
Donna: "Okay, done, Happy Birthday!"
Me: "What do you mean?"
Email alert from cruise line: Itinerary confirmed for The Greek Isles from Venice

Did I mention that my sister is awesome! But I digress. This trip was filled with incredible adventures, immensely beautiful scenery, perfect weather, and a little sister-to-sister bonding.

Our initial port for embarking on this adventure was Venice, Italy. Upon arrival, our epic journey met its first detour. You see, in Venice, the city is made up of waterways as opposed to streets. At first, this sounded pretty fun. However, in order to get around on these waterways, you have to navigate a series of ferry boats in a fashion similar to the New York City subway system. Each ferry operates in a different pathway, to different stations, with some connectors and some direct routes that skip important stations. As you board the ferry juggling various pieces of luggage, you are herded about rapidly like livestock jockeying for position. While my sister and I thought we were well-versed in public transportation, we underestimated this task. After our third encounter with the dockhands at the same station, almost an hour into what should have been a ten-minute boat ride, we realized we should have gotten on the boat going in the opposite direction. We laughed and then finally set a correct course to our hotel next to the iconic Rialto Bridge.

We took full advantage of our short stay in Venice and started to explore the city as soon as we checked into our hotel and dropped off our bags. We walked across the bridge to a quaint little café to indulge ourselves in the most delicious fare of pizza and bruschetta. After lunch, we made our way around the cobblestone walkways and made our first of several stops for homemade Italian gelato! I am pretty certain we took complete advantage of every gelato stand that we passed by, and each taste was even more mouthwatering than the last. We concluded our afternoon with some sightseeing and shopping before heading back to the hotel for a little rest before dinner.

One of the most rewarding hacks I have learned from my sister over the years is the importance of spending time investigating and researching your dining experiences. With a little bit of effort, you can often be treated to tantalizing grub and genuine local hospitality. This was absolutely the case with our dinner selection that evening. After winding through the labyrinth of cobblestone walkways and over countless footbridges, we reached a tiny little hole-in-the-wall family restaurant. We were greeted at the entrance with a smile and glass of wine then escorted to our table. After reviewing the menu, we placed our orders and immediately began to dip our fresh bread into liquid gold oil so that each crevice was submerged.

I learned that evening that one does not simply *eat* dinner in Italy—one *experiences* dinner. I have heard many people talk about the customs of an Italian meal but never quite understood why this was such a big deal until that night. In a word: togetherness. Sitting in that rustic Italian establishment, we felt like we were a part of the family. Conversation amongst everyone in the room flowed as freely as the wine. Through the meal, the chef visited us several times, each time engaging and welcoming. Each trip to our table brought with it a new item from the kitchen that he was excited for us to try. Mind you, we had not actually ordered any of these items, but he exuberantly offered them on the house for his new family.

During each visit, he seemed to become more and more excited as if he knew that this incredible feast of approximately eight courses was about to culminate in the most decadent curtain call to date, freshly made Venetian tiramisu! It was as if a little taste of heaven anchored itself to my spoon.

This, of course, was washed down with limoncello and cookies. How can you not love dessert to wash down dessert?

After dinner, we did the only thing one must do when in Venice: go for a sunset gondola ride through the canals. Typically, this enchanting boat ride is romanticized in movies where some happy couple smoothly floats across the interconnected waterways while the gondolier serenades them with harmonic melodies. It's true. This does happen in real life. We witnessed several apparent couples living out this fairy tale scene. My sister and I went for a little bit more of the parody version, as evidenced by our rapping gondolier and my sister's interesting photo pose with her head bent into the bent crook of her arm while raising the opposite arm out straight in a parallel direction. That's right, my sister was "dabbing" on the gondola. To be honest, it was absolutely hilarious and made for such a fun ride.

We spent the next day touring more of Venice and the small island of Murano. We enjoyed good food, fine wine, and even learned a little bit about the practice of glass blowing. All in all, Italy was a great starting point for our seafaring adventures, and now it was time to trade in our small water taxi for something a little more luxurious. After three toots of the vessel's horn, we were on our way.

Odysseus' first destination after he left Troy was the land of Cicones, where he stopped for food and water. Our initial stop had a similar objective as the cruise ship pulled into our first port of call: Kotor, Montenegro. This was a beautiful little place tucked away in a tiny little region of the Adriatic Sea. During disembarkation, my sister and I took to the land and made our way through the countryside in search of nourishment, just like Odysseus and his men. However, our fate was a little more favorable.

After about an hour's travel, we entered through the gates of the largest vineyard in all of Europe, Plantaže Winery. The vineyard is home to three wine cellars, one of which is housed in in an underground aircraft hangar. As we walked through the hollowed space, gentle conversation echoed about as the aroma of aged grapes and woodsy oak filled the air. After a short period of exploration, my sister and I nestled up to a barrel-turned-table-top set with an extravagant array of charcuterie and wine. We sampled our way through the hues of airy whites and earthy reds. With each small sip, the velvety liquid lingered on my tongue before inducing a suckling descent across my palate.

Although it was tempting to ravage the lands and take home an endless supply of this deliciousness, we thought it better to bow out gracefully while we still maintained our wits, or some semblance thereof. A few photographs in front of the monstrous barrels, one last indulgence of sweet red nectar, and back to the ship we went. It is written that Odysseus lost many of his men during that first trip ashore. While I cannot be certain, our crew did not suffer the same fate. We made a few quick stops to sightsee before we boarded the boat and set our course.

As the week progressed, my sister and I enjoyed many adventures through the Adriatic Sea. Traveling to many lands, each with their own unique parallels to that epic journey that Homer shared. We traveled to Corfu, Greece, where we ventured into the hillside villages for endless views of the dramatic blue sea. At least, I think they were endless. The blurred vision induced by my first interaction with ouzo, a strong and traditional Greek aperitif, made it hard to confirm.

The iridescent blue waters of Corfu gave the stark contrast of the whitewashed walls adorning the cliffs of the volcanic island of Santorini. This latter small island wraps around the edges of an underwater crater and has beaches made up of an assortment of red, black, and white lava pebbles that slope downward into the sea. As we ventured into the small touristy region, we were engulfed in a crowd of individuals bustling through the tiny pathways between walls. If you are someone who is claustrophobic or has significant issues with personal space, this is probably not your scene. Nonetheless, if you pick up the gauntlet laid before you, you may be rewarded with one of the most iconic treasures on "the gram," a picture of you amongst the infamous blue domes. Remember back to that initial message to my sister; this is the picture that started this whole adventure.

After picking up a few trinkets from local artisans, we headed to a restaurant for a traditional Greek meal, celebration, dancing, and customary plate smashing. The most interesting thing I learned on this excursion was this custom was born out of deceit. Our tour guide explained that breaking plates was actually a way of warding off evil spirits during a time of joy and celebration. Smashing plates could mean that the individuals involved were angry and upset, and therefore the evil spirits had no reason to intervene and steal away the joy. Smashing the plates would ultimately fool the spirits. Interesting story and honestly a lot of fun to experience, but I would highly recommend avoiding the use of grandma's favorite china.

Opa!

Next, we traveled across the sea to what many said was the most popular island in the Cyclades. Similar to Santorini, the island of Mykonos was quite picturesque with its whitewashed houses and blue domes. Unique to this island, though, were the gorgeous and vibrant colors of the doors and windows as well as the poetic row of windmills that rest upon the lower hill overlooking the region. Positioned at the ready to harness the winds. In total, the island boasts home to sixteen of these iconic constructions. I presume this is in some way connected to the nickname "island of the winds."

Tourism is prevalent on this island, but the vibe seemed more relaxed in nature. Additionally, not lost on me was the amount of LGBTQ-friendly establishments, evidenced by the plethora of rainbow and pride signage posted around the island. The people were friendly and outgoing with a little bit more of a laidback nature compared to the previous island's crowd. The waterfront was quite the welcoming spot, with its share of cute boutiques, little cafés, and enough bars to serve libations to all who gathered.

My sister and I spent some of our time on the island exploring and learning about the churches and the history. We are both big into history, so this was quite a fitting use of time. After our guided tour was complete, we both spent some time venturing off on our own to explore the seaside. Utterly certain that my sister was taking advantage of the artisan's boutiques, I made my way across the island toward those windmills.

Right off the side of the hill where the windmills held their ground, there was a clustered formation of rock and craters that provided a little opportunity for an abbreviated scrambled hike down to the water. As I started my way down the cliffside, I found an opportunity to sit and take in the serenity that surrounded me. What a magical place. Never in a million years would I have dreamed of being in that position. Sitting there, looking out over the crystal blue waters of the Mediterranean Sea on an island with so much enchantment and mystique. In that moment, I could not help but embrace how profoundly present I was. I closed my eyes and felt the soft soothing breeze dance across my cheek. I felt the warmth of the sun embrace every inch of my flesh. I felt an inner peace that I have rarely experienced and almost never acknowledged. In that moment, I felt still, and I embraced it.

Often in life, we can be fooled by the expectations we place upon ourselves. We sometimes feel that to live means to do more: more work, more travel, more tasks. What I learned on that cliffside in Mykonos was that sometimes we are deceiving ourselves. That all of the "doing" takes away from our ability to actually live presently. Maybe, just maybe, we need to make it a point every once in a while to stop the "doing" and just be still.

I left the island of Mykonos (my favorite thus far) with a feeling of refreshment and enlightenment. It was as if the winds themselves had spoken to me, and oh, what wisdom they had shared.

The rest of the cruise brought forth more scenic villages, incredible cuisine, and pleasant interactions with tour guides and island inhabitants alike. We ventured to the limestone cliffs of Argostoli on Kefalonia to take in the charm of the largest Ionian Island. My sister and I had flashbacks of our Venice gondola as we boarded a tiny little paddle boat to tour the Cave of Melissani set to the musical serenade of our row-master George. Unfortunately, there were no ad-lib dance moves from my sister during this excursion. Uneventful, yet beautiful nonetheless. We concluded the day with a wonderful sunset from the front deck of our suite before making way to our final port of call.

One of the main themes of the Odyssey is the devastating impact of war. This was something I did not make too much of a parallel to when thinking about this metaphor for our cruise. That changed with our next port of call.

The next morning, we awoke to yet another day of sunshine and sensational weather. My sister and I spent the morning enjoying a little breakfast and coffee prior to hearing the bellowing horn sound as we pulled into the medieval city of Dubrovnik, Croatia. Prior to our arrival, I did not know much about this town aside from pop culture references thrown at me regularly by my friends every time I explained where I was headed.

Interestingly, this day was a stark contrast to the upbeat, plate-smashing, happy-go-lucky, libation-induced vibe in all the previous locations. This country appeared more so as a country still navigating its way through the tragedy, grief, and destruction of civil war. This was notable given that well over two decades had passed since the Croatian War of Independence met its conclusion in 1995.

Our tour guide told us stories of how she went to school one morning and was playing with her best friends, and the next day they were mortal enemies. She talked about what it was like growing up for nearly five years and witnessing bomb strikes and building collapses while dodging bullets. How lives were under siege, and many were caught in the aftermath of a city run down by tanks and armies. It was evident in the emotions she shared and the muteness of expression on her face that she had not and likely would not ever recover from the trauma of it all.

After touring the walls of the city itself, which was beautiful despite its past, we made our way out into the deep countryside for lunch and entertainment at a preserved vineyard. As we pulled up to the estate, the architecture was what I would describe as a cross between a quaint Tuscany villa and a medieval European castle. We were greeted at the door and offered a tour of the grounds.

During the tour, we entered a cellar area that had evidence of some structural damage, nothing significant or so it appeared. Then our guide showed us a book of photos that she had curated, providing insight into the degree of destruction and ruin that took place on her land during the war. Once again, the emotional impact resonated throughout the walls. I remember feeling overcome by a sense of sadness in juxtaposition to a degree of feeling fortunate that I had not experienced anything like what they had lived through. These emotions were similar to emotions I felt when touring exhibits at the Holocaust or 9/11 museums.

The enormity of it all was not lost on me. I could feel the deep ache within my chest. The chill of the cold, somber loneliness that was left in the aftermath. My hands trembled, and my voice grew quiet as I silently observed the pain that swarmed around this woman as she shared her story. There was this eerie breeze that blew through the cellar as if it were the breath of those lost souls she spoke of. Her voice echoed off the hollow walls despite the dampening crowds of people intently listening to each word. All connected by a universal compassion and understanding of grief. I imagine these sensations have played out similarly for so many, in various scenarios, across vastly different worlds, through folklore and history.

We must acknowledge these emotions, honor them, give them space, but not be consumed by them. We must find a way to still find the joy in life after devastation.

After the tour, we entered a large gathering room where we were met by two men dressed in suspenders, one toting a guitar, the other an accordion. These fellas definitely brightened the mood with their boisterous humor and musical styling. The emotional aftermath felt like that of attendance at an

Irish wake. Toasts, libations, and a few drunk guys singing, dancing, and clapping. Interestingly, they did a good job of playing to the crowd, as evidenced by an audience-accompanied rendition of "Take Me Out to the Ball Game." After a few touristy pictures, we made our way back to the ship to close out our journey and head home.

As I reflect on the epic adventures and journey through the Aegean Sea, I can't help but wonder, what did Odysseus learn from it all? What impacted him the most? Did he feel the burden of war like those individuals in Croatia? How about the joys of celebration like the crowds dancing in the banquet hall in Santorini? What did he think about in those moments of stillness? And what visions of beauty lingered in his memories… was it the views of the sun rising over the islands or setting over the sea, was it the taste of the wine or the smell of the sweet grapes or was it the people that he met along the way?

I think for me, it's a combination. I hope that through life, we always find a way to embrace the beauty that exists and the moments when it comes to us. Sometimes it's in the chaos, sometimes it's in the pain, and sometimes it's in us, and if we search for it, it's always around us.

CHAPTER 10

FIRE AND ICE

"Once we start believing that the apocalypse is coming, the amygdala goes on high alert, filtering out most anything that says otherwise."

—PETER DIAMANDIS

There I was at the airport feeling lightheaded, nauseous, palms sweating. My heart was pounding through my chest with the booming sensation of a mallet striking against a base drum. I could almost feel the adrenaline coursing through my veins. I thought to myself, *Please don't make me empty my suitcase.*

In 1996, Daniel Goleman wrote a book entitled *Emotional Intelligence: Why It Can Matter More Than IQ.* In this book, Goleman describes a process by which our brain perceives information and formulates our response in one of two ways: rationally or irrationally. Seems simple right? Interestingly, the area of the brain that gets the opportunity to weigh in first, the amygdala, happens to be the irrational side. The amygdala releases neurotransmitters in our brain that help trigger our physiological response to stress. This can sometimes lead to an extreme over-reaction. When this occurs, our body kicks in to fight-or-flight mode without a sense of rational regulation. Often, it's well after the reaction that we actually realize how extremely irrational we have been. Goleman refers to this response as "amygdala hijacking."

Over the years, I have come to realize that my amygdala can be very overpowering. Imagine a boxing match between a 275-pound heavyweight champion (the amygdala) and a twenty-four-pound toddler (our rational cortex). While toddlers can be strong-willed and formidable, I'm pretty sure they would still succumb to the knockout blow of a heavyweight champion. In my case, regrettably, my amygdala holds the title.

Don't get me wrong. Sometimes this is a good thing… you see, the response to this phenomenon is not always negative. You can also have a euphoric overreaction at times as well. Many of my friends have witnessed this firsthand when the most mundane "dad-joke" can send me roaring into a fit of uncontrollable laughter. In fact, my friends quite thoroughly enjoy this reaction and continue to stoke the amygdala further until I am in a fit of hysterical laughter, gasping for air with tears literally streaming down my face. They have dubbed this the "I'm crying" reaction. And boy, does it bring them joy to incite it.

Unfortunately, the "amygdala hijacking" has also led to many not-so-good circumstances as well.

Iceland is by far one of the most beautiful places on earth, filled with so much natural wonder—from cascading waterfalls flowing almost mystically out of the earth and down the sides of luscious green hills to the stark white oversized bodies of crystallized ice that float weightlessly across the glacial bays. This was the perfect setting to get away from the hustle and bustle of the crowded world.

When planning this trip, I contemplated what would be the best way to explore this country without constraints and timelines. After all, given that it would be July, there would be endless sun and plenty of hours to really see what the country had to offer. The idea of being bound to checking in and out of hotels really didn't seem practical, but I am also not one for hitchhiking and pitching a tent. I remember watching a YouTube video about a couple that decided to find a happy medium and explore the country via a camper van. This was intriguing to me. The idea of a warm place to sleep, unlimited mileage, and room for a travel partner seemed kind of cool. So, I picked up the phone and texted my favorite travel buddy, Jennifer!

> Me: "Okay, so hear me out..."
> Jennifer: "okay?"
> Me: "Hiking a glacier, exploring waterfalls, and relaxing
> in the evenings with a glass of wine and s'mores."
> Jennifer: "YES!"

I was not surprised by this immediate response. Within a few moments, the flights were booked. We spent the next few days picking out the van and planning our adventures. Who knew there were so many different layouts for a camper van?

When the day arrived, we loaded up our backpacks and started off on our adventure. If you have followed along with this year of adventure, you have probably noted that airports always tend to give way to some great stories. This trip was not going to change that. When we arrived at the terminal in Newark, New Jersey, we waited patiently in line to go through security. Excitedly, we scanned our passes, showed our identification, and bustled forward toward the conveyor belts with bags in hand. When doing my research, I learned that dry food and snacks would be quite expensive in Iceland, given that most everything is imported to the country. So, naturally, I decided to plan accordingly.

As I placed my bags on the belt, I heard the gentleman from TSA announce some guidance out loud. You know the usual…

"Take all electronics out of your bag."

Sure!

"Take off your shoes and place them on the belt."

Done.

"Take everything out of your pockets."

Perfect, good to go…

"If you have food, please take it out of your bag and place it in a bin for inspection."

I'm sorry, what?

Did he really just say what I think he said?

Consumed with a slight case of amygdala hijacking, I felt my heart rate increase exponentially with a degree of extreme embarrassment about what was about to happen. My face suddenly exuded an immense degree of heat that one could mistake for a fever. My hands trembled as I reached for the suitcase sitting atop the conveyor belt.

I looked at Jennifer.

She looked at me.

The anticipation caused us both to burst into a fit of laughter. I unzipped my extremely overstuffed suitcase and proceeded to dump its entire contents into a bin:

Box of spaghetti
A half Dozen bagels
2lbs of Twizzlers

Two dozen granola bars
Two boxes of fruit snacks
Large bag of sour watermelon candies
Bag of chips
Bag of pretzels
Box of tea bags
Canister of coffee
Bag of sugar
Six pack of chocolate bars
Two bags of marshmallows
Box of Graham crackers
And a bunch of other random snacks.

The TSA agent raised his brows, shook his head in bobble-head fashion, and approached the bin with his little wand. If I had to guess, I'm pretty sure he was a little impressed at our selection. Once cleared through the metal detector, we made our way to an open space on the floor to collect ourselves.

Upon arriving, we grabbed a few bottles of wine from the duty-free shop, picked up the van, and made a quick trip to the grocer to supplement our dry goods with some additional food before heading off on our adventure.

Iceland is known as the land of fire and ice, but this clash of elements creates a unique natural reaction related to water. Across the island, there is water everywhere in many forms, from the boiling geysers to the frozen peaks of the glacier, and all of the powerful waterfalls that come directly out of the hillsides as if Mother Nature is running her fire hoses through holes in the cliffs. We were looking forward to taking in a few of the famous waterfalls along the way.

It wasn't too long before we made our first stop on the south coast, Seljalandsfoss. This waterfall jets directly off the edge of a cliff with a bit of a cavern behind it, allowing individuals to actually disappear behind the wall of water.

Jennifer and I donned our waterproof rain gear and made our way out across the grounds and up to the hillside spout. As we neared the gushing falls, I could feel the escaping mist start to tickle across my face. The rush of the water grew louder and echoed against the cavern as we made our approach. As we came to the false wall of water, I quickly pulled out my selfie stick, and Jennifer and I proceeded to engage in a magical photoshoot with the liquid drops pelting against our raincoats. After a brief moment, we offered our joy-filled gratitude to the earth with a verbal proclamation of thanks and an exuberant hand wave to the magnificent waterfall. We then went on our way back to Van-essa. This was what we named our traveling home.

Our second stop was Skógafoss, one of Iceland's biggest waterfalls; it displays an aquatic descent of almost two hundred feet and spanning over eighty feet across. This enormous fall could be seen easily from Van-essa's windshield all the way from the main road. What is even more fascinating about this natural wonder is that it could also be viewed from the top, as a steep wooden staircase leads to an observational platform above the falling waters. Jennifer and I made our way to the wooden planks and initiated our climb. Upon reaching the observation space, you could see out over the luscious green spaces for what appeared to be an endless horizon of terrain. We explored the upper landscape for a little while before heading back down to face the falls head-on. Needless to say, Jennifer and I felt very tiny; our stature at about five foot five and five foot six respectively was no comparison against the backdrop of the giant cascade. A mighty view, to say the least.

Once back at the van, we set up shop to cook our first meal, a light lunch of frying pan burgers accompanied by a warm cup of freshly pressed coffee. I must admit the freshly pressed coffee was definitely a staple throughout the trip. After lunch, we cleaned up a bit and made our way farther along the south coast, stopping at various tourist locations along the way. One of the best things about Iceland was that each natural attraction was not crowded with people. In fact, there were many stops where it was just Van-essa, Jennifer, me, and the herds of sheep that seemed to wander the land at leisure. This made for a very relaxing vibe.

It was as though we were making our way through wildly enchanted meadows where we often wondered if the only other inhabitants were mythical elves and trolls that would emerge from the feltlike moss-covered hillsides.

One blog entry by Áslaug Torfadóttir from the website Iceland Travel entitled "Elves, Trolls and Monsters" claimed, "If you sit at a crossroads on Midsummer's Night the Hidden People will approach you and offer you gold and jewels. If you resist the temptation to accept, your wishes will come true. However, if you don't, you will be driven mad." We wondered if we might find ourselves propositioned and if we could resist the temptation. So many folklores that provided a series of fun thoughts that truly sparked our imagination.

Over the next few days, Jennifer and I embraced our adventures with wonder and childlike abandon. By day, we frolicked through fields of green and climbed to peaks of glaciers. We raced the top of the basalt walls to escape the grasp of sneaker waves that crept up onto the black sands, and we surrounded ourselves in a crowd of washed-up ice cubes the size of cars on Diamond Beach. Jennifer and I shared the driving duties as we made a path directly across the south, from the east coast of the island to the west, taking in all that that magical land had to offer. One day we traded our land-based vehicle for a water-bound raft to explore the chilly waves of the Jökulsárlón Glacier Lagoon. Then we sought out a stark contrast in climate as we waded in the geothermal sea waters of the Blue Lagoon.

Each day brought with it something new to experience, each night culminated with a glass of wine and a great meal courtesy of Van-essa's kitchen, and each morning started with the perfect cup of coffee against some of the most picturesque views. There is nothing quite like waking up at the foot of a glacier or the base of a waterfall. Turns out van life isn't so bad!

As we concluded the trip, we rewarded ourselves with that soak in the Blue Lagoon to help ease the aches and pains that accompany a few days of sleeping on the not-so-soft mattress of van cushions. This was a really cool place. Unlike most geothermal pools, the composition of the Blue Lagoon is different than anywhere else in the world. We were told by the staff that the combination of seawater and silica does wonders for rejuvenating the skin (although it's horrible on the hair). The long soak in these vitalizing waters was exactly what our bodies needed after our adventures. As a bonus, with our admission to the spa, Jennifer and I also received a complimentary facial treatment. Picture it: the scene in the movie *Mrs. Doubtfire* when she doesn't have her face on, so Robin Williams slams his head onto the top of the cake only to come out with a face full of icing. That is exactly what everyone looks like as they are walking around the lagoon with their silica facial. Nonetheless, it was quite refreshing.

After the Blue Lagoon, we dropped off Van-essa, bidding farewell to our majestic exploration vessel, then headed into the city of Reykjavik for lunch. After a few hours of traversing the city on foot, we closed out our trip with one final night's stay in a hotel before making our way back home.

The trip was truly one of my favorite experiences and being able to share the adventure with one of my childhood friends made it that much better. But then there's that amygdala I was telling you about…

When we landed back in Newark, New Jersey, we were hungry, tired, and exhausted beyond comprehension. I was looking forward to getting back home and recuperating. After spending the week in Iceland, where temperatures barely required us to change out of long sleeves, we did not anticipate making landfall amidst the extreme heat wave that was hitting the East Coast. This would not have been much of a problem but combine the dreaded heat with the limited functional status and impeding jet lag, and that makes for a not-so-great mood. We quickly began to remove various layers of clothing to help thwart the heat, but it was not much reprise. To make matters worse, we had a one-hour train ride still to endure. Luckily, it was just an hour, and we could sleep on the train, so it wasn't too bad… or so I thought.

What I did not realize was the train station was not the typical centralized station like the one we left from. Instead, we were held up on a destitute concrete platform with a very limited aluminum seating to match the unmanned aluminum turnstile. The odor that filled the air was reminiscent of dirty gym socks. There was no place to grab a snack or a drink (which was probably for the best since there were also no bathrooms). All of this was alarming, but what was even more concerning was the complete lack of air conditioning!

As if all of this wasn't enough, there was no worker or service agent to assist when the kiosk would not accept our confirmation number to release our tickets to ride. So there we were, standing in the overheated, nonventilated train station, with nothing to quench our thirst or satisfy our hunger, and the ticket kiosk was rejecting every attempt I was making to get our tickets.

Enter, amygdala!

At that point, I was in a panic; I just wanted to get the tickets, get us on the train, and get us home. While not the best situation, it did not appear to be life-threatening, however my amygdala thought otherwise and threw me into the most exaggerated fit of fight mode. I called customer service at the airline (the airline had booked the train ticket) to figure out what was going on. Inside I felt horrible and embarrassed because I had made the original travel arrangements, and now it was screwed up, and my amygdala was telling me, *This is the end of the world.*

In my communications with the agent, I needed my confirmation number, but of course, it was in my email, which I could not access while I was on the phone. UGH! So, I turned to Jennifer to ask for it, however, when I couldn't see her in my immediate vicinity, I felt even more of a panic. I had to hang up, get the information, and call back. In the midst of that, I found my friend, and instead of calmly and nicely taking accountability, I became defensive and upset with her for not being available to assist. Oh, the irony! I wanted so badly to make sure all of our arrangements were good to go so that Jennifer did not have to stress about it, only to create even more stress by my defensive overreaction.

After finally getting the situation sorted out, I was still reeling so much from my hormonal adrenaline response that I dropped Jennifer's ticket on her lap and walked to the other side of the train platform, and sat down alone. Talk about a passive-aggressive response. Yikes! To compound the situation, our train was extremely delayed, so what I thought was going to be a five-minute alone time turned out to be almost an hour. After taking my seat aboard the cool, air-conditioned train, I started to come down off the extreme overreaction. Unfortunately, the damage was done, and I was consumed with an immense feeling of guilt. Jennifer and I did not talk for the duration of the trip home.

Once we finally made it back to Jennifer's house, I took a quick shower. As the water washed over me, I grappled with the realization that I had acted like a complete jerk. At that point, I realized that my mind was going to linger on the events of the past few hours, and likely I was going to get stuck on a loop of embarrassment, shame, and guilt. Hoping not to continue to cycle through hijacked emotions, I thought it best to pack up the car and take advantage of the fact that I was likely not going to fall asleep any time soon. I loaded up and, after a brief goodbye, I started out on the highway for home.

Looking back, I wish I had handled things differently that day. The severance of that friendship is still something I wish had gone a different way. I hate that in just a few short hours, all of the incredible memories of that trip became so easily tainted in the midst of my amygdala hijacking.

Every day we are faced with moments of increased stress, moments that set us up for this response, moments that give away our rational control. It is up to us to take it back. It's easy to be overcome in the moment. If you find yourself filling up with exaggerated emotions, I encourage you to pause. Give your brain a chance to make sense of the circumstances as they are, not as you initially perceive. Sometimes we just simply must learn to fight the "fight-or-flight."

CHAPTER 11

FORCES OF MOTION

Gravity is a natural phenomenon by which all things with are brought toward one another. On Earth, gravity gives weight to physical objects, and the Moon's gravity causes the ocean tides. Quite literally, gravity acts upon us all at all times.

When I think about gravity, I find myself reminded of Sir Isaac Newton and his laws of motion. I can't help but draw the connection of those laws to the forces that impacted me along my next journey of world travel and self-discovery. So, what do you say gravity? What direction are you pulling me in today?

As I sit here, coffee in hand, this word, *gravity*, spins in my brain. I can feel it all around me in ways I can't even begin to explain. But what if it stopped? What if this force did not exist to weigh me down, if even for the briefest of moments? Would I fall? Would I rise? What would be the impact of it all?

Sometimes I wonder.

My obsession with this force may seem random, but I can't help but think about it endlessly. You see, this has been a week of rigorous exploration into the forces of gravity. It started with our arrival in the western region of the

Canadian Rockies. Alongside my coworkers, I had decided to take advantage of the season and head to Alberta for some solid hiking. Jaclyn and I landed in Calgary and set out toward Canmore, an adorable little town just outside of Banff.

Keeping consistent with most of my prior adventures, I wanted to try something that I had never done before. In agreement with my travel partner, we decided to take part in a helicopter tour of the region. What better way to take in the sites than from a tiny little capsule hovering through space and held aloft by rotating metal blades? Now, I had only ever had one experience in a small aircraft, and that experience did not end so well, especially for the complimentary plastic bag (if you get what I mean). Fortunately, I had not eaten anything off-putting that day, so I felt like I would be in the clear. After a few signatures on a piece of paper, we were escorted to our "bird" and prepared to take flight.

As the chopper lifted off the ground and took to the skies, I couldn't help but feel mesmerized by the views. What a unique perspective to look at the world below: through the transparent glass that encapsulated us. As the pilot flew through the peaks, he shared stories with us about the rocky formations and their history. He detailed the folklore of the Three Sisters and then went on to talk about the Bow River.

Legend has it that there were three beautiful young ladies who fell in love with three brothers from a neighboring tribe, yet tribal law forbade them to marry. The brothers were not happy to accept this law and so decided to use force and capture the three sisters, causing a major tribal battle. To hide them from danger and protect them from any harm, a witch doctor took it upon himself to turn the three sisters into stone. While he had intended to reverse the spell when the battle was over, the witch doctor himself was killed. Since only he could reverse the spell to return the ladies to their former beauty, the sisters remain in their magnificent rock formation as a reminder of this battle for generations to come.

While the story of the Three Sisters was enchanting and the rock formations were quite a sight, I couldn't help but find my eyes drawn downward to the gorgeous blue river that emerged from the glaciers, flowing all the way through Calgary. The color was spectacular. Imagine a painter combining all the colors of the airy blue sky with the whitewashed snow, creating this gentle and inviting hue of tranquil beauty that ran like blue veins through the land. It was captivating, to say the least.

The guide talked about these waterways and their formation. He spoke of how gravity causes the ice of the glaciers to deform and change over time. He talked about the pressure of the glaciers' own weight in conjunction with the force of gravity which causes the glacier to move or flow downward, creating "rivers of ice." This increased runoff changes the rivers, as well as the land itself. The change impacts all aspects of life around it.

Gravity is such an incredible force.

The next morning, we decided to keep true to the laws of motion.

Ten Mile Hike

Newton's first law states that every object will remain at rest or in motion unless compelled to change its state by the action of an external force (NASA 2021).

We woke up early and made our way to Banff, where we would rendezvous with our other coworker for a day of hiking—ten miles' worth.

Over the course of the morning, we watched the sun rise around us at Lake Louis and scaled the peaks and summits of some world-renowned trails, all culminating with a hike to the Plain of Six Glaciers. Here we stopped to sit and take in the views for a bit. While doing so, nature blessed us with the opportunity to see her forces in action. We watched as the peaks gave way to a phenomenon where chunks of ice broke off from their glacier body, a phenomenon known as glacier calving.

This is it! This is gravity in action!

It was beautiful and poetic. From the thunderous sounds to the delayed free fall of snow and ice followed by a beautiful fountain of water being released from within as if the mountains were crying over what gravity had just taken. Now what was not so beautiful was gravity's impact on me as I attempted to stand on very fatigued extremities. I pushed my hands into the ground beneath me, generating what I hoped would be enough force to power upright. However, my legs had other plans as I came crashing down to my backside in not-so-elegant fashion. A little comic relief for my hiking companions no doubt.

Thanks, Gravity!

Over the remainder of the trip, this term, gravity, and the laws of motion that it acts upon continued to spark my attention. I pondered it frequently. Maybe I needed just a little more understanding of these concepts.

Race to the Finish

Newton's second law states that the acceleration of an object depends on the mass of the object and the amount of force applied (NASA 2021).

After closing our time in Banff, Jaclyn and I headed a little over an hour east to the small Canadian city of Calgary. We would spend our last two days of this Canadian adventure here, exploring the city on foot. With this being the last trip of my year of adventures, I wanted to do one more thing to *really* push the limits. Something that would get the blood flowing and create a proper finishing line for this whole experience. So that is exactly what we did.

It's absolutely astounding how many thoughts can race through your head in less than a minute—46.93 seconds to be exact. The bobsled track record for the day, or at least that is what the staff at the Canada Olympic Park bobsleigh track told us. I'm not convinced that every adrenaline-seeking tourist does not hear this same remark.

I stood in the holding room with my helmet secured, staring intently at the map of twists and turns posted on the wall. I was informed in the moments prior that I would be in first position on the sleigh, so I felt that this brief review might be beneficial in my hopes for survival. Fortunately for me and the rest of my four-man crew, I was not truly responsible for any steering, turning, or navigating. These sleighs had been mechanically altered and were controlled by a trained professional who anchored our vessel from the last position. After a few moments, we were called to the start gate to prepare for our run. Just before we took our mark, I peered over the edge of the start slope with angst and anticipation. I could barely hear the last-minute instructions over the thunderous pounding of my heart. I grabbed my push bar, set my feet, and said a prayer.

I remember coming out of the first few turns thinking, *That was pretty smooth!* Boy, did I get ahead of myself. I hadn't even finished that thought before my head was thrust violently and repeatedly left to right. I could feel the intensity of the G-force take control as we slid up the side of the bank, suspended in time and space for what felt like both and instant and an eternity all the same. Then back across the track and a "tap" to the left with the subtlety I can only imagine would come with getting hit head on by a Mack truck.

This repeated over and over for the better part of the downhill journey. I clenched tightly to my position in the front with a grip that would crush most any handshake. My chin was tucked tightly to my chest as if this in some way could take the burden off of the skull enclosure that was tasked with protecting the very organ that led to this insane decision. My body trembled with excitement, fear, and the pure rush of adrenaline. The forces of gravity were pulling me in every direction and yet holding me in place at the same time. It was one of the most exciting, invigorating, and terrorizing experiences to date, and I had been through some insane things over the past year!

After reaching the finish line and glancing up at the time clock, I reveled in the numbers that illuminated the screen. I elevated my hands to the sky, and an audible burst of energy exploded from my body. My travel mate Jaclyn and I rejoiced. I'm not going to lie, some of my rejoicing was simply related to surviving. As the sled came to a stop and my body began to reacclimate, I couldn't help but think of what we had just done.

Flying down the track, forces pulling us in every direction, with our only hope of making it to the finish line with some semblance of survival and minimal repercussions.

This has an eerily similar presentation to life itself. Is this my hope? To merely survive the forces pulling me, to make it to the end as fast as possible. No, that can't be it. I want more than that.

I want to experience the moments, not let them rush by me. I want to float in midair, not be weighed down by it all. I want to remain whole and intact, not be broken and sad. I want more. I deserve more. I want to be free. And, even if just for a moment, I want to defy gravity—not be bound by it.

While the first two laws of motion really came through on my trip to Canada, I think it is the third law that truly depicts not only this Canadian adventure but the whole year's journey.

Hilltop Reflection

Newton's third law states that for every action (force) in nature there is an equal and opposite reaction (NASA 2021).

What a crazy year it has been, and from the moment I opened that piece of chocolate, my world was forever changed. In the past year, I did things I never thought I'd have the courage or ability to do. I'd gone swimming in caves, walked on the ledge of a skyscraper, went around the world in a day. I'd revisited my childhood joys, went cliff diving, drove a speed boat through mangroves, hiked to beautiful peaks of both rock and ice. I'd cruised the green isles, rappelled down waterfalls, ziplined through a jungle. I'd seen wonders of the world and experienced almost every version of transportation from helicopter to Venetian gondola, to dog sled, to speed boat. I'd hiked many, many miles and swum in many seas. And through it all, I learned so much more than I could have ever imagined.

I've learned that for every choice we make in life, there is an alternative. For so long, I chose to let my excuses direct me, but during my adventures, I consciously chose to go in the opposite direction. This action has caused a chain of life-altering reactions. On my last day of travel, I decided to sit back and reflect on it all.

I was caught in a moment of true reflection as I sat atop a hill on a brisk mid-August morning overlooking the quaint little Canadian city of Calgary. I had reached the finish line of my year of yes with a bittersweet recognition of just how differently I now saw the world. There was a juxtaposition of the life I used to live and the life I had experienced over the past year. I longed for a life filled with world travel but previously never prioritized my desires. And in that moment, after having put those desires into action, I found myself embracing a level of contentment with all the places I had been. I was ready to return home.

Sometimes in life we get a late start… and sometimes, the delay can be frustrating. But maybe the time is meant to give us more time to prepare, more time to see things clearly. Then, when we finally do get on the right road, we are able to recognize the beauty around us and realize that the late start has put us exactly where we were meant to be. My travels meant so much more to me than I can even begin to put into words. And to think, without that piece of chocolate, I might not have booked the flight.

In a world where there are so many reasons "not to," we must take purpose in finding the reasons why we "must." It is easy to get caught up in the excuses: not enough time, no money, too far, too scary, etc., but when you commit yourself to making it happen you will find no regrets. It will challenge you, but it will also change you.

When I started this series of adventures, I did not know what to expect. I can't explain what has come to me in moments like this… moments where I find myself standing on the precipice looking out into the vastness of my own existence. It is in these moments that I feel my happiest and most free. It is in these moments that I truly begin to understand what the universe has to offer. It is in these moments that I find the light within.

I encourage you all to put yourself first, to make it happen, not to let anything come between you and who you are meant to be. Choose to be the action that generates the reactions around you. Be the catalyst and set your life in motion.

PART 2

THE LUST

—

CHAPTER 12

NEW BEGINNINGS

———

There are moments that mark our lives into distinct pieces, moments that serve as a divider of life and time, of who we were before and after. This was one of those moments...

I was sitting in my cozy office with my freshly brewed coffee emitting aromatic vapors into the air as I reflected back on the last several weeks and months. It had been a few weeks since that last trip, and I was still recovering from my year of adventure and travels. I was excited to finally get a little time to unwind and reintroduce myself to the local world that I had managed to escape for a year. Although I was physically exhausted, I felt strikingly rejuvenated. It was as if I had just come back to life after completing my own real-life epic adventure similar to that of the aforementioned Odysseus—minus the war, cyclops, and false presumption of death. I came away from the adventures feeling a new sense of self and excited for what possibilities might exist. The anticipation was exhilarating, and I was on cloud nine.

Since I was finally going to be grounded in one location with a little more free time on my hands, I felt like this was an opportunity for me to reengage myself in the dating world. I had not prioritized dating over the preceding year because I did not want to fall into distraction or disappointment that would impact my travels. I felt the hold was also important because I wanted to use the time for me. I tend to be a person that bends toward the wants and desires of others, and often that means missing out on things that I may want to see or do. This past year was different. I allowed myself to be selfish, and I prioritized my joy, and in doing so, I got very acquainted with who I am and my own likes and dislikes. Honestly, it was quite eye-opening. Turns out, I don't like pasta as much as I thought I did, who knew!

Ready to start reconnecting and putting myself out there, I opened my phone and reactivated my online dating app. You know the kind, swipe right for your heart's delight. I uploaded a few pictures from my travel adventures and modified the profile to reflect the new me. The world traveler, the lover of all things chocolate, the woman in search of kindness, compassion, and an incredible sense of humor. I posted the changes and started to spin the dating roulette wheel. I did not really have any expectations, to be quite honest. I just figured I was in a good place, and the timing seemed appropriate so, why not. I definitely did not anticipate what would come next.

> Hi Devon, you've got me stuck here. I don't know which picture to ask about first! Did you take a personal photographer with you or were you followed by the paparazzi?

And so it began, a random message on my phone from a complete stranger. As I looked at the remarks, I couldn't help but smile. *I remember this woman.* The instant her image first came across my screen, I couldn't help but be struck by those eyes, so captivating and yet intriguing, as if she herself had this remarkable story to tell. Mind you, I had not paid close attention to this dating app, and the idea of an online connection was a bit uncomfortable for me, but there was something about this one. I remembered looking at her profile for several moments before inevitably swiping right. There was a comfort in those playful images of her in relaxed jeans and a green T-shirt, enjoying a little sunny weather and playtime with her pup.

The next image on her profile revealed that same beautiful woman overlooking a foreign city skyline. She had radiating auburn hair cascading over her shoulders in perfect contrast to her surroundings. She stood amidst the bright yellow foliage of what looked like a vineyard that had yielded a lifetime of the sweetest grapes and has now retired, feeling satisfied in purpose. The ethereal woman peered out into the world as if to say *I see you world, all of your beauty and strife, your hope and challenges, darkness and light, and I am here for you.* This particular image, so strong yet soft, was so fascinating and mystical to me as if it was the embodiment of ancient mythological lore. This woman on the hillside, a goddess in her own right with onlookers from below. I wondered what those onlookers saw when they look up to her, how magical and enchanting the stories would be of this woman on the hill.

And now, this woman was messaging me. I was consumed with a combination of excitement and anxiety. *How should I respond to this playful introduction?* After pondering a few responses, I moved forward with charming witty banter.

> Hello Corina (beautiful name)
> I typically recruit a team of twelve highly trained
> photographers to follow me around and take pictures,
> so people will think I'm famous;) just kidding, it's

amazing the pictures you can get with an I-phone, a
remote, and a tripod these days.
How are you this evening? Enjoying a good start to your
week, I hope?

And send.

While I did not have a lot of experience with the whole
dating app business, I had learned that if you are interested,
you should always respond with an open-ended question to
engage the conversation further. The anxiety increased as I
contemplated the response. *Will she think it's cute, or will she
be turned off by my horrid attempt a humorous flirtation via
an electronic device. Were my questions invasive? Did I use
the word "good" in a proper context?*

Ding!
The alert sounds.

Twelve, that's it? You probably need more. I suggest you
take a team of twenty next time.
Today has been pretty good, especially for a Monday!
My rabbit (and I am not a rabbit person) got his paw
stuck in the door while defending my honor against
a spider. He's given me quite the guilt trip all evening.
How did your weekend treat you?

What a response, sarcastic and engaging… and just like that,
the mythological creature ascended from her mountaintop
vineyard and entered into my world.

Over the next few days, I thoroughly enjoyed the
exchange of conversation, flirtation, and banter. There were
more conversations of chivalrous cat antics, worldly travels, food, family, and of course—chocolate. What I did not

realize was how much this woman would come to mean to me, and how I would enjoy getting to know the story behind those captivating eyes.

My father used this awkward expression growing up: "Shit or get off the pot." While a bit aggressive and distasteful, the sentiment made sense. You don't want to waste your time sitting on the toilet waiting for something to happen. There comes a point in the online dating world where you must make it happen or give up on the attempt and move on; get off the proverbial pot.

I had just returned from New Orleans for one of my best friend's bachelorette parties. Corina and I had been talking via text messages for a while now, and with each exchange, the conversations grew deeper and more connected. Now that I was settled in at home and back into my routine, I thought that right then was as good a time as any to explore the possibility and see if there really was a true connection. In the midst of chatting with her over some randomness of the day, I finally shook up the courage and asked if she'd like to meet me for a "quick" drink.

One thing I've learned is that you need to have an escape plan, so if things are incredibly awkward and there is absolutely no connection you will have something that will get you out of there before too much lamentation and torture set in. So, of course, I kept us in mind when I made this plan for our first meeting. I asked Corina if she would like to meet me for a very quick drink on my way home from work. I said the timing would be tight, but I'd be coming through town, and could stop for a bit before heading home to take care of the pup. Corina obliged.

I strategically planned it for that day because usually when I work at the university, I look a little more presentable. I have my hair done, makeup on, wear a little bit more of a busi-ness-type outfit. A power suit, if you will, minus the jacket. I knew that I would feel confident and comfortable, plus I didn't have to worry about the dress code for the evening or the anxiety that comes along with "do I wear a T-shirt, jeans, am I overdressed, am I underdressed" etc. So, we made plans to meet at a cute little wine bar and restaurant downtown.

As I drove down to the bustling area to find parking, I heard the alert from a text message come through my phone. Corina was already at the agreed-upon meeting location and, in what was consistent with our communication, her thoughtfulness came through as she provided me with the precise location where I could find her once I arrived. As I parked the car and began to approach, I could feel the flut-tering of nervous butterflies taking flight inside of me. The wings fluttered more and more rapidly with each step as I walked up the sidewalk to the patio area where she was waiting. The patio was surrounded by beautiful, flowering bushes and lush green trees that blocked the view from my direction. The anticipation was mounting.

I started to feel like an adolescent preparing for their first date. My heart was racing, and I was quite certain the palms of my hands would likely have slid off the handle if I had to open the gate. Luckily, the gate was open, and the path for-ward was clear. As I crossed through, I turned my head. One quick glance across the patio. Our eyes met, and her face lit up in this cliché hopeless romantic-comedic moment where time stops and sappy music subtly fades in with the accom-paniment of birds singing. The butterflies in my stomach had escaped from within and were now converging around us in choreographed flight.

That moment changed everything.

The conversation that was intended to last for about fifteen minutes and one glass of wine turned to a second glass and a third hour. We talked about everything that evening—from her hairdresser who'd intently encouraged her to change from bleach blond to scarlet red, to her exotic name that just flowed off the edge of the tongue like it was accentuating her very identity. We continued with engaged communication, back and forth, feeding off of each other's stories as we crafted this harmonious melody via conversation. There was laughter, lighthearted banter, and there was deep conversation about our families.

Typically, I restrict myself from this type of conversation until I feel completely comfortable to open up, but there is something so organic about the nature of our exchange that I felt no hesitation. One of the most striking moments was her poignant response to my brief declaration about the passing of my mom. Most individuals acknowledge and quickly sidestep deeper conversations around painful experiences—myself included—but Corina honored the topic in the most compassionate and endearing way. She stopped me from my programmed response and gave space for the personal disclosure I had just made. She made me feel present in the moment, and through her reaction, I felt safe to reveal things so openly.

The evening continued forward with an overwhelming ease of expression and communication. And as the glimmering stars took the sky overhead, my escape plan turned into more of an unwelcome deadline, much like midnight for Cinderella. The meticulously calculated minutes turned into magical hours and ultimately, now it really *was* time to get home to the pup. That evening, I met the woman of my dreams, and my life would be forever distinctly divided into who I was before and after I crossed through that gate.

Following that first encounter, the weeks continued to bring with them a degree of joy and happiness I had never experienced. I found myself hanging on every word, moment, and memory that we shared. For the first time in a long time, it seemed that all of the pieces were starting to come together in a perfect fit. I couldn't help but become excited for what was to come.

CHAPTER 13

THE QUESTION GAME

———

"What's one thing you really want to tell me?"

This was the question typed on a two- by three-inch piece of cardstock. The ink boldly staring up at me from a contrasting white background as if to taunt me with my own thoughts. *How do I answer this question knowing what I know? I can't do it. I won't. She will never understand.* There was no explanation, no words I could possibly conjure up that would even suffice. Feeling overwhelmed and tormented by my own device, I hung my head for what felt like an eternity.

Let me take you back to the beginning…

Corina and I had been dating for several weeks, and things were going incredibly well. She's one of the most kind-hearted and thoughtful individuals to have ever walked this earth. When we first started seeing each other, before we considered the relationship "official," we followed all of the socio-normative protocols of getting to know each other. You know, daily communication, late-night conversations, and of course those initial introductions to the friends and fur-babies. It's like the vetting process for human relationships. I always found this quite an interesting experience, likened to that of a human video game with each level a bit more challenging than before. You know the kind where the survivor is rewarded with an acknowledgment from the princess. Now I am hardly a princess, but I would gladly stand in waiting to reward this beautiful woman any day.

Level One—The Friend

Most people may think that the introduction to friends should be a little later in the vetting process, but, to be honest, my friends are the most spot-on judges of character. They are extremely important to me, so if you don't make it through this level, then there is probably no use wasting anyone's time. Being that we were still early into the getting-to-know-you process, it was important for me to see what the vibe would be like in a nonthreatening low-key environment.

It was a refreshing Sunday afternoon in late September. The sun was shining, the sky was a perfect hue of blue, and the breeze was just enough to graze across the green leaves covering the trees. My friends and I were closing out a weekend of celebrating the upcoming nuptials of two amazing people by showering the bride-to-be. What better location to do so than the local brewery?

It was absolutely perfect. Me and others from the bridal party set up a light brunch to provide a bit of sustenance in conjunction with the seemingly bottomless mimosas. The event unfolded seamlessly, and after ensuring all the guests were enjoying themselves, it was time to relinquish my hosting responsibilities and relax.

I was sitting with my friend Julie at the far end of the brewery counter. We were mixing our colorful commentary about the bride unwrapping her gifts with dialogue about this new woman that had been the root of my recent permanent smile.

"Oh look, she must be so excited for that new potholder she can barely contain herself," Julie said with a slight chuckle.

Julie is that hilariously sarcastic friend that is just a tiny bit older and possesses a degree of unparalleled wisdom that makes for perfectly uninhibited mom advice. In my opinion, everyone needs a Julie in their life!

As Julie and I delved further into the conversation, I was just beaming about Corina, so of course, Julie's response was, "Well, where is she? Tell her to come here. I need to meet her." The pale liquid sunshine that tickled our tongues helped reduce the inhibitions that may have otherwise stopped me from extending a post-party invitation for Corina to join us. So, I picked up my phone, and in a matter of moments, it was confirmed. Corina was on her way. "Wonderful!" Julie remarked in an excited voice that also made me slightly nervous. I could only imagine what type of grilling was about to take place.

When Corina arrived at the brewery, I performed the introduction. "Julie, Corina; Corina, Julie." I am pretty sure that was the extent of my facilitation in that conversation. To my immense delight, the two hit it off extremely well. There was one point where I was shooed away from the two as if I was infringing on their outing. Glancing over from across the room, I could hear a light-hearted giggle emerge from them both. A slight sign of relief set in as Julie gave me the nod of approval.

Level One—Passed

The bridal shower had ended, and the crowd of women had dispersed. Many of them made their way on to their next location to meet up with the guys who were watching football at a bar down the street. After spending a bit of time exchanging laughter and conversation, Julie was ready to depart. At that point, I obviously did not want to say goodbye to Corina and therefore extended another invitation for her to join up with the full friend group that had been enjoying their Sunday fun-day a few blocks away. To my extreme delight, the invitation was accepted.

Level Two—The Group

After a short walk, we arrived at the venue where the guys were. There was a nice little crowd enjoying the variety of football games broadcast across multiple screens. This was a perfect way to spend a little time in the company of friends. Laura, the bride-to-be, who was also one of my closest friends, was standing at the bar with several members of our crew. Laura is that friend that wants nothing more than to see everyone truly happy. Her genuine joy for others' happiness is unparalleled and makes for the most welcoming vibe. I was excited for Laura to meet Corina because I knew that she would be so excited too. I was not wrong. She welcomed her openly into the group.

As I stood there with Corina, I could not help but be captivated by the way she carried herself amidst the crowd, engaging with everyone she met. Her voice was so upbeat and her laughter so full of energy. I also couldn't help but feel this sudden strike of electricity each time her body grazed ever so slightly across mine, one of the benefits of a crowded space. It was both electrifying and comforting just the same.

Level Two—Passed

I could tell by the reactions that my friends very much enjoyed meeting Corina, and I very much enjoyed the opportunity for them to do so. As the afternoon started to extend toward evening, I felt myself growing slightly selfish. I was ready to spend a little one-on-one time with this incredible woman. So, after a few moments of goodbyes, we settled the tab and made our way out into the open air.

Corina and I spent the remainder of the afternoon walking circles around the downtown streets, lost in endless conversation. By the time we had made what must have been our third or fourth lap, time was beginning to slip away. We were approaching my car, and although every fiber of my being just wanted to keep walking, it was time to close out the day and make my way home. We stood at the rear of my Jeep, continuing the conversation for a few more moments, both seemingly wanting Father Time to pause and allow us an infinite number of moments to continue on. In those fleeting moments, I could feel an overwhelming desire building inside of me.

Truth be told, I have never been one to make the first move, but here I was standing in front of her, entranced by her, wanting nothing more than to lean in and kiss her. My knees were slightly quivering. My heart was racing. My body flushed with this intense yearning. *Kiss the girl* was echoing in my ear. Alas, all that build up culminated in the most anticlimactic cowardly bow out, remaining sadly consistent in me not making the first move. And if that wasn't bad enough, as I went to step backward and maneuver around to get into my car, I tripped off the curb, nearly falling into an oncoming car. Ugh the embarrassment.

Level Three—The Pup

A few days later, I invited Corina over to my house for dinner. I had recently taken up boxed meal service in an attempt to improve my culinary skills, and it made for a great excuse for requesting company for dinner. To my surprise, my embarrassing antics downtown had not deterred her from accepting yet another invitation. This was promising.

I know I have said it before, but Corina is one of the most thoughtful individuals I have ever met. She listened intently through conversation and picked up on small details that may often go overlooked. Like when she showed up for dinner with a bottle of red wine and dark chocolate truffles! Let me repeat that… dark chocolate truffles! Mind you, our only conversation about chocolate to that point was back during our electronic communications where we talked about the catalyst for my travel adventures being a piece of dark chocolate.

Just when I thought it couldn't get any better, I took note of the energetic and playful interactions taking place in my living room. Typically, when new guests come to the house, my dog is usually a bit too intimidating. People are often put off by his size, his energy, and his unfortunate drooling problem. None of that seemed to be of any concern to Corina. She jumped right into play mode, giving the pup so much attention and joy. It was as though she, herself, had secret powers to tame the wildest of beasts.

Level Three—Passed

Over the next several weeks, spending time out on walks and playing in the park with the pup was something we enjoyed regularly. There was something so fun about those fall mornings with a cup of coffee, a comfy pair of sweats, a few doggie treats, and a brisk breeze blowing across our faces as we walked through the trees, thoughtfully joining our hands on the leash. Those comfortable fall days extended the most enchanting evenings dancing in the kitchen or laying under the stars. I found myself encapsulated in the most intense connection I had ever experienced. And that blunder-filled moment on the curb back in September when I couldn't muster up enough courage to kiss her, well that led to an even more romantic, organic moment shared in private. A moment that opened the flood gates for countless more kisses.

Time and time again, I found myself reflecting on all the thoughtful things she did to show her affection on a regular basis. The progression of our relationship was flooded with small acts of kindness. I had always thought that I was one to really try to find little ways to add joy and meaning to someone's day, but with her, it was a constant back-and-forth. She always made me feel so cared for and special as we continued to grow and get to know one another.

Level Four—The Milestone

As we approached our "one month" mark, we thought, what better way to celebrate than to return to the place where we first met! I was so excited for the evening and could barely contain myself throughout the day. I remember being at work, talking to Laura about my plans for the evening. I had a card picked out and was going to show up with a single long stem red rose. I absolutely love roses. There is something so romantic about a flower that can express all your words and sentiments in something as simple as their color or number. I have always found something so fascinating about the gesture of offering a rose. To me it is like a mystical and secret language shared between two souls.

I explained my plan to Laura. I was going to leave work early to get to the café before Corina and surprise her with a symbolic gesture of my affection. However, in true Corina fashion, the surprise was mine. As I walked in, Corina had already arrived and found a location in the far corner of the room. On the table in front of her were five of the most exquisite flowers that I had ever seen, each one unique in color and shade. An envelope with my name was placed gently over the stems. In that moment, the beat within my heart skipped as though it too was in shock at the expression that had been offered. No one had ever put so much careful thought into curating such a beautiful and delicate display of adoration for me. Each rose represented a different progression in our connection and all together told the story of us. In the envelope were tags for each of the rose colors. As I pulled each tag and matched it to the stem, we pulled up the proflowers website on my phone to explore the meanings of each. The story she had crafted about our relationship was profoundly poetic…

Lavender—enchantment
Purple—adoration
Orange—energy, passion, excitement
White with red tips—unity
White—new beginning, hope

Level Four—Passed

How lucky was I to be the object of her affection? How lucky was I to be a part of this fairy tale that even the romantic literary greats could only dream to pen? Officially being in a relationship for one month is pretty significant in my opinion. It is enough time to start to settle in and see how your lives mesh together. One month was that internal deadline for me where I felt I could have a pretty good grasp on how I felt and if I saw a future with someone. As we hit that milestone, I felt an even stronger pull toward Corina; I couldn't help but be excited for what was to come.

Looking back on that night and the many days and nights preceding, I knew it was inevitable. It was just a matter of time before I would have no choice but to disclose what was weighing so heavily on me. I should have known that I would not be able to escape it. The weight of that disclosure only grew heavier as we approached the final level of our metaphorical video game.

Level Five—The Family

Fall had progressed quickly. It was mid-November, and the Thanksgiving holiday was approaching fast. With it came the recognition that the story we were writing was about to include a few new characters. Corina and I were contemplating our plans for the holidays and had made the decision to move forward with bringing our families into the narrative.

We packed a weekend bag, arranged care for our fur-babies, and headed off up the highway to enjoy a somewhat traditional meal with Corina's family. This was an incredibly big deal in my opinion, as Corina's family had not known about Corina dating women prior to us. My mental preparation was tormented by visions of all the stereotypical coming-out horrors that people read about in the gay rendition of *"my holiday nightmare."*

Leading up to the trip, I had a sense of anxiety. Granted, for the most part, my family experiences had been fairly supportive and uneventful, but I, too, had experienced a horror once or twice. This time carried with it a bit more weight because this girl really was something special, and I wanted it to go well for her. As I said, this was an incredibly BIG DEAL!

Not surprisingly, the induced anxiety fell away completely once we placed our coffee cups in the cup holder, interlaced our hands, and headed off on the highway. There was always something so magical about her touch, how it could be the most energizing and soothing all the same. I felt completely at peace.

The entire drive was filled with conversation, as was typical for us. There was always something so captivating about our conversations. The intention behind her inquiries always made me feel like she truly wanted to see me. It was nice to be seen by her.

Once we arrived at her family's, the chaos of the holiday came to life in the best way possible. I felt such a sense of normalcy around her family and enjoyed getting to know each of them. It was special to watch the dynamic between Corina and her young niece and nephew. How much they lit up in her presence and how overjoyed they were to see her. It made my heart melt in a sense of complete recognition as I, too, felt the same in her presence.

Level Five—Passed

The remainder of the weekend went well, and I cherished the time I had spent getting to meet Corina's family and spending time getting to know them. As the weekend drew to a close, we packed up the car and made our way back home. I remember a very distinct moment where I glanced over at Corina as she was peering through the side window as if lost in a moment of open thought. I remember how inexplicably beautiful she looked to me in that moment, and not from a physical standpoint (don't get me wrong, she is stunning). It was in that moment that I saw this vision of who she was down to her core. This unearthly beautiful soul sitting across from me. It was in that moment that all uncertainty escaped me, and I was filled with a sense of undeniable clarity.

Proceed to Reward

It had been a few months since we started talking, and it seemed like each day brought with it more appreciation for each moment spent with Corina. We had made it to the point where there was a recognition that this was something different. Something magical. And so there I was, sitting in my living room with a subtle soft melody playing on the speaker and the crackle of the fireplace snapping in the background. Sitting crossed-legged on the couch, Corina just an arm's reach away, we were face-to-face with a little deck of cards set between us.

I couldn't help but think about that moment in the car. And the moment in the café, and all of the countless moments where the thought has crossed my mind. I was sitting there, staring at this tiny little card, knowing that I had to tell her. *I've got to be completely honest with her. But how?*

There was no explanation, no words I could possibly conjure up that would even suffice. Feeling overwhelmed and tormented by my own device, I hung my head for what felt like an eternity…

How do you find the courage to say it?

"What's one thing you really want to tell me?"

The answer was clear…

Corina, I love you.

But instead, I cowered and bowed my head as I returned the card to the deck, gathering just enough courage to muster the word:

"Pass."

CHAPTER 14

A NICE RING TO IT

———

*"If you want to have something show up in your life, the
kind of person you would like to become, manifest something new into your life, something powerful, whatever it
might be. You obviously must first be able to imagine it."*
—WAYNE DYER

Have you ever wanted something so bad that you were willing
to go to great lengths to prepare yourself to receive it? I remember as a kid growing up playing sports. We would always say
"when we win" as opposed to *"if we win."* It was as though the
words we said somehow had an impact on the outcome.

I heard the words of Mr. Dyer amidst a not-so-uncommon trip down the rabbit hole of social media video clips
that streamed continuously across my six-inch screen. I was
sitting on my couch, snuggled up my comfiest fleece-lined
hoodie with one hand clasped around the handle of a steaming cup of caffeine. On the big screen across the room were
images of remembrance broadcasting from the memorial

sites of Ground Zero. It was September 11th, 2017—two years before Corina and I met.

I remember being flooded with a plethora of emotions as I sat on my couch that day. Thinking back on the last six years of my life, how much had changed and yet how much remained the same. The video clips on my screen were a welcome distraction from the larger images that I still couldn't bring myself to turn off. It is rather interesting the way technology has developed over the years. It was as though this tiny handheld device could see directly into my soul and, through a calculated algorithm, spit out a series of inspirational compilations that sparked the embers of my innermost reflection. And in a moment, one compilation, in particular, stoked those embers and ignited into flames.

In the YouTube video compilation from Video Advice entitled "You Are the Creator," a variety of distinguished voices provide insight into how to create your life. The video starts with Morgan Freeman's deep husky voice urging us to imagine what life would be like if we could access even 20 percent of our brain's capacity—as if he was challenging us to see that such a small percentage of our focus could change our lives entirely. As the music faded, the voices shifted to Mr. Dyer's voice, and those profound words caught my attention. By the end of the ten-minute clip, this concept of *manifestation* was at the forefront of my mind. This concept that with positive, constructive thought, we could make our dreams and desires a reality. That is, if we really truly believe it is possible, it will happen.

I found myself wanting to explore this further and, in doing so, found myself infatuated with all the ways people have brought their hopes and desires to life. There were vision boards and daily affirmations, silent meditation, and verbal proclamations. And in one instance, I came across a blog post of a single woman that encouraged others to write a letter to their future love. What an odd but unique and interesting approach!

The idea was that in writing the letter, not only were you placing your desires into the world, but you were also examining and declaring who you were and recognizing where you were in your life. Once those words were on paper, you could always refer to them as a measure to ensure that you were holding yourself accountable to your innermost hopes and dreams for your partner. After a few moments of contemplation, I rose from my cozy little blanket cocoon and made my way over to the wooden desk in my office. Equipped with my smoothest G2-07 pen, I began to scribble away on the translucent blue lines of my college-ruled notepad.

To the woman reading this,

I believe to my core that we have the power to influence the universe by what we speak into it. So today, I'm writing this letter to you. I'm writing this before we meet, knowing wholeheartedly that if you are reading this, then all of these words are true. My certainty comes in knowing exactly what I am looking for.

I've been on the journey for a while now, at some points wondering where you are and when I would find you. There were periods of doubt that encompassed me, but the power of your love motivated me. At times when I felt my loneliest, the anticipation of your embrace was comforting. I don't know when or how, but I knew when the time was right, when I was ready and capable, you would come into my life.

You see, it took me a while to realize who I was, to prepare myself to be capable of giving my all to you. I am grateful for the time I spent within myself and for the moments that helped shape me in preparation for this day. This day when I can finally say: I have found the woman of my dreams.

Without doubt or hesitation, without fear, without question, you are the epitome of everything I have ever wanted. You know, there comes a point in life where you search your heart and soul and begin to recognize exactly what it is that completes you. You begin to realize that the waiting will be worth it. When you know exactly what you are waiting for, the idea of settling for anything less is just unacceptable. And in that moment, suddenly, it all makes sense. You begin to feel excited to wait because you finally understand that you are waiting on "the one."

The one that you will love forever, the one who will see you for who you are and love you in ways that empower you to be the best version of yourself. The woman that will challenge you to see the world in new ways and bring you joy beyond your greatest expectations.

As I write this letter to you, I can't say for certain the color of your eyes, but I know that looking into them will be one of my favorite things. And I can't draw out the shape of your lips, but I know that I would do anything to make you smile.

You are the absolute of me. My heart, my soul, my world. I am eternally grateful that the stars aligned, and the forces of nature placed you into my life. I love you, for all that I know you are. For everything that you

make me want to be. I love you beyond understanding.
Beyond reason. And I am so incredible thankful that
my journey has finally, finally led me to you.

Two years later and was sitting outside of this quaint little jewelry store rereading this letter that I sat down to write a little over two years before. A letter to the woman I would marry. When I wrote the letter, I had not met her yet, but I knew on that day without a doubt that it was just a matter of time. What I didn't know is that she would come along and exceed everything I could have ever dreamed of. Corina brought so much meaning and happiness into my life. She challenged me to see the vibrant colors in places that previously appeared gray. She stood by my side in moments of sadness and disappointment, celebrated with me in times of joy and success. She made the little moments matter and made space for the big moments. She loved me unconditionally and taught me that fairy tales are real. I felt so incredibly lucky that the universe read my note and brought her into my life.

Sitting there with that folded letter in one hand and a velvet-trimmed box in my other, I thought to myself, *Did I really just do that!* My hand was trembling as it held that tiny, hinged box. The object inside was glistening, with each ray of sunlight dancing across its surface. The stones were aligned meticulously around the winding peak and hugged tightly together and secured within the embrace of white gold. I was struck by this vision and what it represented. The promise that it would hold. The promise of unconditional love in the times of happiness and joy, and times of disappointment and sadness. The promise of encouragement and support. The promise of each tomorrow.

I thought about our relationship. Poignant moments crossed through my mind like images on the screen. I was overcome with a visceral emotion. It was overwhelming, the recognition of just how lucky I was. It was the simple moments that repeated with distinct detail. I closed my eyes. I could smell the scent of her hair as I remembered that first dance in the middle of the kitchen floor. I could feel the chill of her skin as her nose brushed against my cheek laying wrapped up in each other's arms in the hammock under the stars. I could feel the butterflies swirling inside of me, just like they did the moment our eyes first met.

Of all the places I had been and all the incredible adventures I had been on, there was nothing more exhilarating than being with her. She had placed meaning into the moments of my life, and I could not wait to embark on this next adventure with her by my side.

Now it was time to manifest another "yes."

Our subconscious mind is a powerful thing. It's important to recognize the implications of our thoughts and how they will alter the course of our lives. We must be careful to pay mind to the thoughts we think and the words we speak into the universe. If you are unhappy and miserable, chances are that cloud of darkness will remain attracted to you. If you are exuberant and full of life, seeing the world through the lens of positivity and hopeful in your proclamations, you might just reap the benefits of those thoughts. It's natural to have moments where we feel defeated, alone, and hopeless—but we cannot live in that self-deprecating world with reckless abandon. We must take charge; we must put forth the energy that we want in return. We must call out for our most pressing wants and desires and then make space to receive them.

CHAPTER 15

THE SILENCE OF IT ALL

Have you ever planned or been part of a secret surprise for someone? In order for there to be success in the surprise, there is always an element of silence. Shhhh… keep it a secret. Don't tell anyone. Quiet everyone, here she comes. Have you ever wondered what's in that silence… and can a little bit of a silence really make a difference?

We had been back from a few of our vacations for a few weeks, and life was rushing back in. With work and schedules, Corina and I were managing as well as possible between all the demands. Recuperating was the biggest thing on the horizon; at least as far as Corina was aware. For me, I could barely contain the excitement for all the plans I was about to set in motion over the coming months.

Back toward the start of our relationship, Corina and I had the most intimate conversation during a Sunday outing down at a local vineyard. I remember that day vividly. The hues of yellow, orange, and amber leaves reflected of the mirrorlike surface of the vineyard's pond. There was a crispness to the warm breeze as it blew in from across the fading lily pad leaves. Corina and I sat perched in the folds of our respective wooden Adirondack chairs, positioned next to each other at the water's edge.

As we sat alternating between sips of wine and open dialogue, we began to discuss the future and what ours would look like. We talked about the prospect of children and both our hopes and fears related to the rearing of little ones. We talked about our families both through their impact on our lives, and the way their roles and perspectives may alter and shift nebulously over time as our relationship became more visible to them all. We talked about our hopes and dreams.

It was in the midst of that conversation that I confidently declared I was going to marry her one day. We both paused with that particular statement, not in hesitation, but rather with a calming recognition of accuracy. It was as though we both knew the connection that had existed between us was undeniable, and ending up together was inevitable. I could feel the warmth fill my cheeks as I looked into her eyes and the peaked edges of her smile gave a resounding confirmation. What an incredible feeling it was to find a sense of completeness after such an extended length of longing.

That vineyard, and that spot by the water, has remained one that I am very fond of. The enormity of that conversation that punctuated our relationship in a way that bred forth a fairy-tale. I think back to that conversation often, and I remember the stillness that existed for us there in those moments. It was a place where I felt our journey began to unify. So much so that I had hoped to return to that precise spot and make good on that proclamation.

I was going to bring her to the water's edge and ask her to marry me.

But first, the preparation.

Now, back around Christmastime, Corina and I had both entertained the idea of looking at engagement rings on multiple occasions. We had spent evenings on the couch running through image upon image of rings and settings on our phones. We even utilized the imaginative technology where you can hold your hand to the lens and virtually "try on" the ring. It's amazing how far technology has come. At any rate, I was still of the old-fashioned mindset of seeing a ring in person. So one night, Corina and I decided to take a ride across town to a few jewelry stores to get some ideas.

I must admit, ring shopping with her was one of the most adorable experiences. It had been a cold dark evening, and I wore comfy jeans with a warm coat. Corina was in a salmon-taupe-colored leather jacket with a matching winter beanie adorned with a little puff ball on the top. I loved the way she looked in that cute little hat, innocent and angelic all the same.

As we sat down at the counter, the sales associate began to bring a series of rings forward for Corina to try on. You could sense the anticipation as the associate encouraged her to pick them up and try them on. Corina delicately lifted the first tiny piece of precious metal from the velvet surface to get a glimpse of the sparkling aesthetic. She smiled intensely for several moments, peering at its beauty. She then attempted to return it to the safety of its padded bed.

Unfortunately, the nervous excitement caused her to bobble the piece of jewelry slightly so that it fumbled out of her hand onto the glass casing. A slight gasp of embarrassment and horror quickly eased by the reassurance of the sales associate that there was no way the slight mishap would cause damage. We laughed and continued to look at all of the beautiful pieces put forth.

Since that initial trip, we continued to look at rings intermittently. At times, we were together, and at other times we were doing our own investigating and sending pictures of our findings to one another.

During one of my own attempts at research, I visited a local jeweler to look at a few pieces in their store. As I grazed across the cabinets, I was drawn to the style, sparkle, and simple elegance of one ring in particular. From the second it was pulled from the glass casing, I knew it was the one. It was subtle in its banding and different in the diagonal staging of diamonds around its setting. The prominent diamond was sunk almost flushed to its surroundings while still commanding the light through its size and laid protected by its adjoining stones.

I had the sales agent write down the description of the piece as well as the identification numbers for it on a business card that I securely tucked within my wallet. She agreed to hold the piece aside as I made arrangements to confirm it would be suitable for Corina.

Later that evening, I took Corina to that little family jewelers to look across their selection. As she glanced over the pieces, she decided to try on about three different ones. I could barely contain myself in the background as her eyes connected with the piece I had admired previously. After several moments of making googly eyes at the piece, we handed it back to the agent who placed it back into the display, and we made our way to the stores exit. Unbeknownst to Corina, as we left the store, the agent pulled the ring from the display and set it aside for me to complete the purchasing process later that week.

Now, Corina is not someone that relishes super expensive flashy jewelry. She is practical and subtle, which I adore. I also recognize that wearing a pricey engagement ring can bring with it the stress of knowing you have said ring on your finger at all times. In an attempt to mitigate some of this stress as well as offer a token of my desire to build a life with her, I decided to present Corina with a small promise ring. Something to hold the place where soon the engagement ring would sit.

Corina wore that promise ring constantly, and seeing it on her finger always provided me with a sense of hope for what the future would hold. The promise ring also provided me with a bit of time to prepare for what I could only hope would be a very special proposal.

Even with knowing I had a little time to prepare, the anticipation was mounting with each day. There were often days where I would wake up and had to talk myself out of just dropping to my knee over morning coffee. I mean, the simplicity of that might actually have been appreciated by her, but the truth is she deserved the romantic fairy tale moment—and I wanted to give that to her. But first, there were a few other special moments I needed to prepare for.

You see, Corina's birthday was just around the corner, as was Valentine's Day. Unfortunately, these events fell right in the midst of a trip and conference that I had committed to attending. I wanted to do something special to mark the occasions, but doing so from hundreds of miles away was going to take a lot of planning and a little bit of help from a few others.

The week before, Corina and I would enjoy a wonderful Pre-Valentine's Day date night. Drinks, dinner, and a show. Then, while I was away for the week, my best friend Laura would secretly deliver a special birthday cake from a local baker. This was the same cake that Laura had at her wedding, and Corina absolutely melted over the deliciousness of said cake, so of course, it would make for a fabulous birthday cake. Another benefit was that Corina, who absolutely dreads the thought of burning candles on a cake, would come home to a wonderful cake surprise minus the fire and off-key singing that usually accompany a birthday cake.

Upon my return, we would spend the weekend in full celebration of her, starting with a surprise guest visit from her best friend as well as her sister, a day of girl time. Then we would close the weekend with a limo and winery tour with friends. Now the trick was to keep this all a secret from a woman who could probably double as a private investigator if she wanted to.

Unfortunately, over the course of the plan's execution, several circumstances began to unfold that wreaked havoc on the scheduled events for the week. Instead of a flawless week of celebration, it became a week filled with mishaps, tension, and frustration culminating in communication breakdowns and stress.

I must admit, I do not handle stress very well at all! Especially when things start to fall off course, and I sense a loss of control over a situation. This is that strong amygdala response all over again. In the wake of disarray, I found myself becoming short and abrupt with Corina, essentially defeating all the purpose behind my plans. To make matters worse, I had somehow become quite ill, first with cold-like symptoms, then fatigue, followed by a nice little visit from a respiratory infection. During a time where I so just wanted to put to focus on this beautiful woman and celebrate everything about her, she was left to worry and take care of me. Instead of her spending the week feeling loved, adored, and cherished, she spent the week feeling worried, frustrated, and

utterly drained. This was not what I had planned; nevertheless, I proceeded forward as best as I could.

When I was trying to put together this extravagant
agenda of events, I started to lose sight of the point behind
it all. I became so consumed with pulling off the perfect surprise and making sure everyone else would enjoy themselves
that I stopped paying attention to the only person whose
opinion and feelings should have mattered the most. But in
true Corina fashion, she went along with it all. The birthday
weekend came and went. However, despite what seemed like
a good time, something seemed a bit off. I couldn't quite
pinpoint it. Maybe I was still a bit under the weather, maybe
Corina was a little put off by my well-intended deceit, or
maybe it was just a bit of winter depression. I wasn't quite sure.

In the weeks after that, I started to feel a sense of discon-
nection set between us. For some reason, I was still struggling to find my energy, and with our schedules becoming
more and more conflicting, Corina and I were spending a lot
more time apart. During this time, I felt like a piece of me
was missing. We would still FaceTime each night before bed
and catch up intermittently throughout the day, but things
were hectic. Our weekends were off as Corina had started to
pick up some time with some classes she was teaching, and
I was on a variable schedule with commitments for both of
my jobs. I figured once we made it through the chaos a bit,
we would settle back in and start to feel more like ourselves.
There was nothing that could stand in the way of us getting
back on track, or so I thought.

Enter…

A global pandemic!

Are you kidding me? Not only were we a bit disconnected,
the world had to go and throw a global pandemic into the

mix. It was like the universe was taunting us. No place to go, nothing to do, and the weight of the world consuming all outlets of media around us. And to top it off, the tension between Corina and I had hit an all-time high; our phone interactions and FaceTimes were riddled with discontent and more frustration. As tensions mounted, insecurity started to rear its ugly head. Thoughts of self-doubt and unworthiness began to torment me with each day that we spent apart. How could this be happening? I was literally sitting there looking at her engagement ring, planning out the details of a proposal, all the while feeling so far removed from the magic and passion we had come to know. While on the phone with her, I found myself thinking about that ring and wondering for the first time if she would say yes. The insecurity of that moment was crushing. I couldn't quite explain it, but tension started to become palpable and, in an effort not to disclose my thoughts, I excused myself from the call with a statement of avoidance when she inquired about what was on my mind.

In an effort to calm the thoughts of insecurity and make time for us to reconnect, I planned a fun evening at the house for the two of us. I cooked dinner, set up a makeshift movie theater in the spare bedroom, and turned the empty walk-in closet into a private home speakeasy equipped with a full self-service bar and twinkly lights (because who doesn't like twinkly lights?). It was time to shut off the news, turn out the lights, and just embrace the present moment with the woman that I love. It was going to be perfect, and I was very much looking forward to finding our way back to the us that I had come to know.

The evening seemed uneventful, we finally were able to spend some time with each other, and it was incredible to see her smile and feel her presence. Overall, it was a nice evening together, and as the evening drew to a close, Corina helped me carry some of the dirtied glasses from the "bar" down to the kitchen to clean up. We weaved in and around each other in the kitchen, but something seemed off. Typically, our bodies always seemed magnetically pulled toward one another in that space. Soft subtle brushes as we skidded behind one another. A gentle graze of the hand across the small of the back when rounding a corner. That night though, it was as if we were out of sync. She leaned in as I turned. I reached out as she unknowingly backed away. Perhaps I was overthinking it all.

While sitting there at the kitchen island, Corina posed a question about our phone conversation from the previous evening...

"So, what was it that you didn't want to say last night?" she innocently inquired.

"It was nothing really. We can forget about it," I responded.

But it wasn't that simple. As Corina inquired further about my reluctance, I couldn't help but disclose the insecurity and frustration I had been feeling lately.

As I disclosed my thoughts and feelings, the heat of the conversation started to build. For several moments we went back-and-forth, analyzing how the last several weeks had been unfolding. Each verbal profession of our perspectives was countered by a defensive proposal of the intent. The words became more fueled and emotional with each volley back and forth.

Corina's feelings versus my intention
My feelings versus Corina's intention

Back-and-forth, over and over in the verbal equivalent of a championship tennis match, each statement and reflection causing us to chase farther and farther across the court. Until finally, one inquiry was lobbed into the air...

"Do you want to be with me," she asked.

A million words crossed my mind, a flashback of every moment of our relationship to date, all the hopes and wishes and dreams. The thought of the little velvet box inside the drawer was merely one room over. Everything on the tip of my tongue ready... I was ready to send the final spike across the court and declare my unequivocal love for this woman without question and end this relentless back and forth.

And in that precise moment as she lobbed those words into the air, ready to meet my proclaiming spike...

Silence.

As if the ball had fallen from the sky and quietly bounced across the finish line, echoing with each tap of the rubber to the floor.

"Your silence says it all," she remarked as she removed the promise ring and placed it down on the cold hard granite surface. The sound of the precious metal clinked softly in contrast to the shattering of the promise that it represented. The sound pierced through my heart. This wasn't what I wanted. Not at all. My silence was not an indication that I wanted out, but in retrospect, I recognize that the passive-aggressive impact of that silence spoke volumes. She deserved better.

In that moment, my head and heart sank into defeat. *What just happened? What did I just do?* I fumbled with my words, backtracking to make some semblance of sense, but at that point, the damage was done.

And just like that, words I was so certain I would never hear from her.

"We are broken up."

There comes a point where you cross a line that you can't uncross. When your actions have consequences, and your words, or lack thereof, carry with them more than you may be able to comprehend. I will never truly understand why I hesitated, why I held back, why I didn't say the words that I knew Corina needed to hear. Was it self-sabotage? Maybe, but that doesn't make it right. When we live in a constant state of insecurity, we place an undue amount of pressure on those around us. Sometimes, if we are lucky, the ones we love withstand the pressure, but is that really fair? Is that love?

Sometimes, hard as it may be, it's what we hear in the silence that matters.

CHAPTER 16

LIKE MENDING BROKEN GLASS

How do you pick up the pieces when the shards are so sharp that touching them will likely cause you to bleed?

The night of the breakup had been gut-wrenching and tumultuous. After the moment of impact set in, I recall sobbing and pleading hysterically for her to stay.

She didn't.

We attempted to try and talk through the emotions of it all in the days after and did our best to grapple with the gravity of the situation, but that only led to a cyclic loop of more heartbreak and pain for all parties involved. I swayed back and forth across the line from "sure, we can be friends" to the "you hurt me so bad I resent you" mentalities. There were moments of hopefulness for a return to our previous state of unequivocal bliss, only to then be offset by the gut-wrenching recognition of how different things were.

In the immediate weeks following our breakup, we still talked daily and made attempts to spend time together several times a week. Of course, I took this as a sign of interest but ultimately realized it was more of a placation. Subconsciously, there were still weird forces of nature that existed around our connection. We could go a few days without talking, and then randomly, I would have an intense dream urging me to check on her, which somehow typically seemed to coincide with moments when she was upset or needed a friend. It honestly was a bit unnerving.

Initially, I tried to do everything I could to make more of a concerted effort to show her how much she meant to me without expectations for reciprocation in any way. One day, I woke up two hours early just to drive out of my way to surprise her with coffee because I knew she had a big interview first thing in the morning, but I left it outside her door so as not to interrupt her morning routine. Despite all the pain and anguish, I still genuinely wanted to be a semblance of comfort and source of good in her life. Hearing that, in some way, my minor inconvenience made her day better was something that brought me contentment.

We would get together pretty frequently still. I was working on being a bit more adaptable. Instead of always hanging out at my house, I would load the pup in the car, and we would head out to her place for breakfast or for dinner and a walk. There was something about spending time with her in her place, her world, that just made me smile. To be honest, I spent a lot of time wondering why we hadn't done that more often. Truth was, she never asked, and I never offered.

Lesson learned: relationships require equal effort, even in the little things.

There were so many points in those first few weeks after we broke up where it seemed like things were going so well again, and then there would be the inevitable moment of resentment that would set in. How could things be like this, but we weren't together? That was ultimately followed by the realization that it shouldn't require prompting by heartbreak for us to make more of an effort. We both deserved more than that.

While some moments seemed to go well, it was clear when we hit that period of frustration and resentment in the cycle, it would become brutal. I am someone that has a difficult time holding in my emotions, and Corina is quite the opposite. This contrast served as a catalyst for my insecurities. The more insecure I became, the more emotional my response was. This insecurity was also something that contributed to the demise of our relationship.

Couple all of this with a slew of outside influences—a growing global pandemic, longer lockdowns, job stresses, and personal loss—and you have a recipe for disaster. The emotional meltdowns were becoming taxing for both parties, and it had finally reached a climactic breaking point where we just had to take a break.

"Six weeks," she said.

"Six weeks, how did you come up with that, Corina?" I echoed as my insecurities mounted even further.

Obviously, six weeks would turn into forever, and that would be the last time I would hear her voice on the other end of the line. I was convinced this was the last exchange we would have. Despite the feeling, I conceded. And with one last hope for reassurance, I asked, "Are you really going to call?" My voice quivered in doubt.

"Yes, in six weeks, I will call," she said without hesitation. "We need time. We need space."

She wasn't wrong, and I knew it. This didn't stop me from fearing the worst outcome. This woman who I had come to love, this person who had become the largest part of my life, would now suddenly be gone and likely not return.

"You know I'm scared, right? I don't want to think about a life where you are not a part of it," I said. She nodded her head and, reluctantly, I agreed. "Okay, Corina, six weeks."

Knowing me better than I would have cared to admit, she repeated her proclamation. "I will call you in six weeks," she said confidently to reassure me one last time before we said goodbye and hung up the phone.

I was shredded. I sank to the cold hardwood floor of my kitchen and sobbed buckets of tears into my sleeves until the late hours of the night. I felt a chill as I moved the wet fabric of my garment across my face. With eyes swollen and no more tears left to cry that night, I staggered my way up the stairs to put myself to bed.

To say the next several weeks were hard would be an extreme understatement. I tried to force myself to stay busy, but it didn't seem to give reprieve from the pain that sat within my chest on a daily basis. I started a new job with the hopes that the transition would serve me well, and I forced myself work out regularly again. While all these things might seem beneficial, I still felt like I was just going through the motions. The only thing that seemed to bring solace was the unwavering support of my friends. My tribe of friends that stood by me when I couldn't find the strength to muster on. I relied heavily on them to get me through the emptiness that consumed me.

My friend Cassidy (the one from the Dominican Republic) would do virtual game nights with me regularly. She is the kind of friend that lets you cuss like a sailor and vent every emotion you need to without judgment and then provides you with immense validation amidst the best sarcastic humor. My friend Laura (the happy bride) would meet me for rainy day walks when I just needed a break in the silence. She is the steadfast friend that would do anything to ease your pain. And my friend Julie (the wise one) would make sure I was eating by regularly encouraging me over a plate of appetizers and Mexican food. She always offered the best experiential wisdom and reflection.

My friends encouraged me to reconnect with who I was. Each day got a little bit easier, but every day was still tough.

I remember watching the days on my calendar tick away, knowing that I needed to start moving on and letting go. As the six-week mark approached, I realized that the likelihood I would hear from Corina was slim to none and that I needed to be okay with that.

I tried.

It was still hard to think of having someone whose mere presence made your life exponentially better suddenly dissolve from their rightful place. How difficult it was to fathom having someone who meant so much just completely disappear from your life. To say I was struggling was putting it lightly.

But then, in a single moment, I felt my heart pause.

When I saw the phone ring, I didn't know what to say or think or feel. Instantly in that moment, I reached for the phone, and I froze. *It's her!* She was calling. And after what felt like an eternity, I slid my trembling finger down the surface of the screen and across the little green icon to accept the call.

"Hello?" I said in a wavering, timid voice as if answering in any other way might scare her off.

"Hi." Oh… the sound of that *hi*. It was a sound I knew so well… a sound that both calmed me and haunted me all the same. "I don't really know what to say, but it's been six weeks, and I told you I would call."

Somehow, we talked for nearly three hours that day. The conversation was filled with a unique compilation of happy sadness as we caught up with each other's lives. It was bittersweet to hear how much had changed for us both in such a short period of time. I had started a new job. She was going to be moving. We had both been navigating the residual effects of our breakup the best we could. Despite the pain of our past, the dialogue flowed just as easily as it had that first night at the café. Time was lost, and for the first time in a very long time, I felt content in the space that our words occupied.

That conversation led its way to future conversations. Initially, it was as though the conversations were spaced out in accordance with a logical and safe schedule as if this would provide a degree of protection to our hearts, but inevitably they started to increase in frequency. The content of conversations evolved from light, small talk, and recaps of the day to the occasional dive into more profound and thought-provoking conversations. At times, we could recognize a glimpse of the connection that had once existed while all the same, we would find ourselves mourning the loss of that connection in our own ways. After several phone conversations, things progressed to video interactions, and eventually, we even agreed to a friendly dinner.

Not surprising, given how natural our ability was to connect in the beginning, our dinner conversation spread into the late hours of the evening and well beyond the food and wine. We laughed and interacted with a level of playful innocence that set the foundation for which we would continue to see each other in person moving forward. Over the course of the summer, we worked our way back to a steady place of safe interaction, both of us doing our best to navigate the waters of friendship.

As the summer started to end, Corina was coming closer to the deadline for which she needed to find a place to live. She did not want to stay in the same area, citing too many memories coupled with what I could only imagine was a sense of stagnation. I didn't fault her for this thought process. Truth is, I had contemplated a change of scenery myself quite frequently since our relationship ended. My fear was that this impending move would once again take her out of my life and impact the friendship more than just logistically. Still, it was not my place to generate an issue for her; after all, it appeared she had been under enough stress with it all. So I tried to do what any good friend would do and offer all of the support that I could, including singlehandedly moving the world's heaviest treadmill down a flight of steps while in business clothes. That's what friends are for, right?

Trying to maintain a friendship with someone that you have loved so deeply and significantly is about as easy as trying to captain a sailboat under the windiest of hurricane conditions. With Corina's impending move and a strong desire to connect with someone again, it was only a matter of time before we both had to make our attempts to move on. In an article on Medium, P. G. Barrett repeats a well-known quote attributed to Zig Ziglar that says, "Most people stand on the dock of life waiting for their ship to come in when deep down inside they know it has never left port." This sentiment resonated with me. As with most boats that head into open waters, the sea was not always as calm as one might have hoped. Just a short period before the move, Corina had made it known to me that she had started talking to someone.

Hearing that from her felt like the sting of a serrated knife across the skin. What could I say?

I guess I had to face it. Corina moving somehow equated to us moving on.

We had both eventually ventured into the world of dating others. For me, this was a difficult process. The idea of meeting—let alone dating—someone new was absolutely terrifying. And to even muster the thought of her with someone else literally made me sick, like full-on vomit. But neither one of us wanted to hold the other back in any way. Well, I guess that's not true. I much would have preferred she never date again, but that is not realistic, and ultimately, I did want her to find happiness. I just wished it could have been with me.

The most difficult parts of this moving on process were the comparisons and residual letdown. No matter who I met or how great they were, they were never her. And that made for quite the complication. How do you find the woman of your dreams and then not compare everyone else to them? Impossible, in my opinion.

And then there is the nagging recognition that with each step you take in the direction of something new, there is this tiny little voice hanging out in the back of your mind holding a sharp shard of your broken relationship, attempting to hand it over to you with that tormenting thought…

"But what if there's still a chance?"

CHAPTER 17

SURVIVING THE FALL

——

"The new year stands before us, like a chapter in a book, waiting to be written."

—MELODY BEATTIE

New Year's Eve 2020

I came into the past year filled to the brim with the light of a thousand stars illuminating the nights sky. My heart was exploding at the seams with more love than I could have ever contained. So excited for the future I had longed for with the most magnificent woman.

So much has changed. It had been a while since that night when my world shattered to pieces. The year was coming to its end, and thoughts of hope for a new tomorrow were at the forefront for so many.

A new job, a global pandemic, and a broken heart later—I was just happy to make it out alive.

As the year drew to a close, I sat down to put my proverbial pen to paper and gather my thoughts in to some semblance of coherency. I wasn't sure if I would ever know why or how I got so far away from who I was: at home, at work, with her. I knew that I could not change what had happened in the past. I could only learn from it and grow forward. I promised myself I would go into the new year with a new perspective based on transparency and self-truth. I wanted to see it as a fresh start, full of the new opportunities and endless possibilities, but I recognized that in order for that to happen, I needed to honor and grieve the losses of 2020.

A wise woman once told me that it was okay to hold space for those not-so-great feelings. So as the sunset on another year, I decided that was just what I intended to do.

I was sitting at my kitchen island with a few pieces of chocolate and a half-empty glass of the smoothest red wine. The surface of that sweet scarlet liquid reflected the flickering candlelight that danced within its own glass enclosure, almost in perfect synchronization with the soft and subtle music from the Echo speaker that filled the air. The melodic tones brought with them a slew of fervent memories. To my left sat a box of tissues, well within easy reach, and to my right, there was a box filled with pieces of her. How do you pack up so many magical moments knowing that you are packing away so much joy and happiness, likely to never revisit them again?

On the table… I was greeted by the first pictures of us starring back at me from atop of a pile of love letters and little notes. As I read through each carefully curated word, a flood of heartbreak washed over me like I had been hit by a tidal wave, left struggling to tread the water, gasping for breath.

Leading up to that night, the fatigue of it all set in. My heart was heavy and aching. My body beyond the point of utter exhaustion. I was simply tired. Tired of the fight. Tired of the hangover that seemed to linger after each interaction with her. Tired of the torturous contemplation of what could have been and what went wrong.

I felt my body giving way to the powerful forces that crashed over me for so long. I sank below the surface with nothing left. Completely submerged in an ocean of sadness and dismay. And as if I hadn't been beaten enough, the music, forgotten but still cycling through songs, began playing a melody I knew all too well. It was the same song that had been playing during that first slow dance in the kitchen and a thousand times thereafter. In that moment, my body began to quiver with weakness, fatigue, and sorrow. I felt all aspects of the life I had come to know slip away. The ocean of despair consumed me, and I was thrust deeper and deeper with each bombarding wave until, finally, I had nothing left. I felt myself weightlessly drifting away from the anger and sadness that I had felt.

I existed only in that moment, numb and lifeless.

Still and paralyzed, I listened to every word. The montage of our relationship played itself out on rewind in my thoughts. The memories, the passionate moments, the subtle glances, yet still I could feel nothing. My mind, reminiscing on our time together, continued its span through each moment, working back to that first glimpse from that café.

But it didn't stop where I thought it would.

The visions kept going back to all of those moments before her. Those moments where I was tested and scared of what the future had in store. Moments where every fiber of my being was screaming for me to retreat. Moments where I was forced to come face-to-face with all of the choices I had made and the excuses I had provided. Moments where I was so consumed with what was that I could barely see what could be.

Moments of complete and utter disappointment.

I saw that girl sitting there clenching a leather-bound, unused passport in her hand and wondering what had happened. How did she get so off course? And then I watched her unwrap that tiny piece of blue foil that encapsulated her chocolat—and in that instant, everything changed.

The montage suddenly shifted direction and began playing forward, giving me the opportunity to watch as the story unfolded before my eyes. The moments started to show a girl triumphantly taking control of her life, navigating her way through adventure after adventure. I started to see the flatness in her expression morph into peaks of permanent smiles, beaming with excitement. I saw her learn to find the beauty in all that surrounded her. I saw the montage of her experiences come to life as she transitioned from a shy, fearfully inhibited persona into an outgoing, resolute, and vibrant being. The girl that waded the waters to introduce herself to strangers, the girl that leaped from the mountaintops and tamed the waterfalls. The very same girl that rounded the fence corner at a little café with confidence and excitement for what the future would hold.

The video clips began progressing into focus with the most vibrant colors. And as the frames continued to come into view, I felt a single tear trickle down my cheek, leaving a definitive path as it made its descent. I could feel it. I could feel all of it, I could see it… the colors came to life growing ever more vivid and intense.

I didn't understand it. What was happening? In that moment, I felt different. I felt free.

I saw a girl fall in love, but this time, it was not with the person waiting in the café courtyard.

This time, it was with herself.

As the song faded away into silence, I emerged from the surface of the heavy waters. And almost instantly, I came to life with a new degree of optimism and hope, knowing that I was ready to let go, to appreciate my past for what it was: my past.

It had been so easy to get caught up in the bad stuff. To let my mind wander down this path of what we didn't get to do, and all of the things that never happened. It was easy to think about all of the sad moments that echoed on repeat, but that night was different. That night I just felt so incredibly grateful for my time with Corina and for all of the magic that existed during our moments together.

For so long, I avoided those memories and cast them to an isolated oblivion in the back of my mind so as to not breakdown. But that night, I gently placed those memories in that faded brown cardboard box and smiled for the first time in a really long time. The anger dissipated, and the sadness faded into the night.

I sat and embraced the feelings as I remembered how much love we had shared. How much that woman on the hillside infiltrated my heart in a way that I never had felt before. I thought about how much she loved me and I her. Sometimes, in the midst of the brutal anguish, it was easy to lose sight of what we shared. In such a short period, she gave me a love I never thought possible. Now it was time to find a new love.

I thought about how many books adorn my shelves thanks to the poetic masters of McWilliams, Thomas, and Neruda. Their words forever etched within my mind. Poets that write of the most earth-shattering, gut-wrenching, romantic love. Love so deep and profound that simply reading the words of such professions can bring forth a yearning for something more. I was not sure that I could ever truly comprehend the magnitude of that love, but it's the kind that changes you to your core. A love that takes you to the brink and then brings you back again.

There is only one problem.

Most people think that a love so profound can only come from someone else—but this is simply not true. If we are being honest, truly honest, we will see that the deepest and most rewarding form of love can only come from within. In that moment of truth, I realized that it was time to love myself. I was ready to move forward so that I could begin crafting the story that comes next.

I thought about the moments where I had felt the most present, the most connected, the most understood. The moments where I felt a true purpose for my existence in this universe were the moments where I let go, gave in, opened up, and set myself free. It was in those moments that I had the courage and strength to stand alone and where I learned that the purest love I could ever feel could only come when I learned to love myself.

The universe has a peculiar way of teaching us these quintessential lessons. The problem is, we need to take the time to receive its instruction.

April 2021

It has been three years to the day since I opened that foil-wrapped piece of chocolate. To say that the last few years had really been a roller coaster for me would be the most ridiculous understatement. I think about everything I have learned during my year of yes, and how those lessons were paramount in my survival during one of the worst years of my life. The interesting thing is, those lessons were not unique to those events in my life. In fact, they are lessons that have been staples throughout my entire lifetime, repeated through a variety of perspectives, each carrying with it the innate ability to reel me back in to the recognition of what truly matters. The problem is, we get so caught up in the act of living out the minutes of our life that we really do take for granted our own ability to truly become our life. The ability to transcend through the timed components and really experience our existence. I believe if we make a conscious effort to hold ourselves accountable for who we truly are, then it is inevitable that we discover a life that is so much more than we could ever imagine.

Now, I do not want to provide a false front; I realize that I lived through an extravagant year of yes. I recognize that not everyone is in a position to just drop everything and hop on the next flight. That's the beauty of it all. The lessons that I have shared with you along the way are everyday lessons that can fit into any area of life. You don't need a sunset over the Aegean Sea to remind you to be present in the beauty that surrounds you, and I would strongly advise against hurling yourself out of a speeding sled. All you need is to do is be open to what the universe is trying to tell you…

The Last Page

Be kind. Be kind to the agents in the terminal, be kind to the people that surround you, and always be kind to yourself.

Stop holding yourself back with excuses. There will always be a reason not to do something. Too busy, too tired, too much. I challenge you to question the validity of those statements.

Open yourself up to the possibilities that the world has to offer. Let them challenge you. Let them change you.

Let go of your fear. You can spend your time filled with so much anxiety that you never leave the ground, or you can take a deep breath and let yourself have the courage to fly.

Find comfort in the company. Whether it is in the friends you keep, the memories of loved ones passed, or the crowd of strangers that welcome you in. These connections will fill you up and allow you to see the world in a different light.

Roll with it. Things are not always going to go as planned. At times you may feel completely out of control. It will be okay.

Don't let your moments of regret consume you. You are going to make mistakes, hurt people's feelings, and even let yourself down. Acknowledge it, accept it, and allow yourself a little bit of grace.

Know your worth. Find a way to honor the relationships in your own life, and most certainly cherish them, but don't forget to prioritize yourself. You matter.

Be grateful. Appreciate the path you have traveled, the people you have met, and the impact they have had on you.

Hold on as long as you need to, and then, when you are ready… let go.

Give yourself permission to be free.

Free to laugh.
Free to feel.
Free to love.
And free to experience whatever adventure comes next.

Stop living the life that was written for you, and start writing the life that you deserve.

ACKNOWLEDGMENTS

This book journey has been a cathartic, reflective, labor of love. Writing has always been a method that allowed me to process through the circumstances of my life, but this book has gone far beyond that. Sharing my story has pushed me beyond the realm of comfort and allowed me to find the courage to be authentically me. I started this process, but WE made the story become something so much more. If you have enjoyed this creative work, please know that it would not have been possible without the help of so many others. Words cannot begin to express how grateful I am for all the well wishes, encouragement, messages, social media likes, and support that I have received throughout this process.

First and foremost, I would like to take a moment to thank a very special coworker whose encouragement pushed me to write this book, Amanda Couture. I told her that when I published my book, I would be sure to make note of her in my acknowledgments. While it may seem small, that conversation was motivation to ensure I kept true to that statement.

I would also like to thank Professor Eric Koester from Georgetown University. His guidance and enthusiasm made this process fun. The continued encouragement from Professor Koester and the Book Creator community helped me believe that this was possible. I would like to also thank the team at New Degree Press for their efforts and support in bringing this book to fruition. Specifically, Asa Lowenstein (my developmental editor) and Sarah Lobrot (my marketing and revisions editor) for their insights and direction that helped bring this story to life.

Special thanks to my team of reviewers, Karen Applebaum, Meghan Bergman, Tammy Blackburn, Liz Carlone, Jamie Kerr, Sarah Hetzell, Brynne Parmele, and Jessie Wright.

I would be remiss if I did not say thank you to the many travel companions that gave way to the hijinks and shenanigans that brought color to these pages: Cassidy, Leiselle, Stacia, Tiffany, Patricia, Juliet, Donna, Jaclyn, Laura, and Vicky. The stories that fill these pages as well as those that were left untold will be memories that I treasure always.

Thank you to KRE for the reminder that the story doesn't end when the page turns.

Thank you to my niece Lauren for your adventurous inspiration.

And finally, I would like to take a moment to express my gratitude to all of the friends and family that supported me during my presale campaign and helped to make this dream a reality.

Hilary Aderman
Nina Arrington
Jennifer Bailey
Logan Barbour
Jamie Bastable
Pepichek Becker
Caren Begun
Meghan Bergman
Tammy Blackburn
Emily Bressner
Chelsea Butler
Breanna Campbell
Lizz Carlone
Jennifer Carmichael
Patricia Clay
Ken Comstock
Amanda Costanza
Amanda Couture
Carrie Craver
Amanda Crum
Holly Daube
Bonnie Deblois
Bailey Ditty
Sean Donnelly
Jamie Dasilva
Ayesha Eatman
Lisa Eickholt
Dave Ellerson
Denyse Ellington
Farris Fakhoury
Nadya Fedun
Amy Fick

Adrienne Fiumenero
Mari Furr
Johny Garcia
Wendy Garrow
Julie Ghormley
Jess Goodine
Jourdan Gray
Taylor Guardalabene
Stacia Hall
Shauna Hartshorne
Becky Helms
Sarah Goyette Hetzell
Laura Hilliard
Katherine Hughes
Bonnie Jackson
Meagan Jarvis
Elliott Johnson
Stacey Juliano
Jamie Kerr
Eric Koester
Nicole Kriske
Sennette Krug
Lori Leineke
Cathy Leonard
Jeff Liano
Lisa Willis Litaker
Julie Mayberry
Colleen McCart-Reymer
Leah McCoy
Rebecca Medendorp
Skylar Metzel
Michelle Meyers

Terry Miller
Mica Mitchell
Amanda Mittelstadt
Marie Moffett
Laura Nix
Happi Overton
Maureen Perno
Cassidy and Keith Pilston
Liz Poole
Jaclyn Redman
Karen Reimiller
Dominique Reynolds
Tanya Robinson
Aimee Rogers
Christy Ruszala
Jill Sawyer
Mathew Sawyer
Jesse Scinto
Cheryl Scully
Robin Anne Severino
Steve Solecki
Karen Sweeney
Kellyn Taylor
Linda Vanartsdalen
Jessica Vann
Katy Walton
Susannah Washburn
KellyAnn Weaver
Donna McCart Welser
Neisha Wetzel
Dawn White
Dean Williams
Jessie Wright
Jamison Young

APPENDIX

Author's Note

Gandhi, Mahatma. *The Collected Works of Mahatma Gandhi*. Volume 13: January 1915—October 1917. Govt. of India. New Delhi: Ministry of Information and Broadcasting, 1964.

Gilbert, Elizabeth. *Eat, Pray, Love: One Woman's Search for Everything Across Italy, India, and Indonesia*. New York: Penguin, 2007.

Gilbert, Elizabeth. "Me & Rayya." Facebook, September 7, 2016. https://www.facebook.com/GilbertLiz/photos/me-rayyadear-ones-there-is-something-i-wish-to-tell-you-today-something-which-i-/1107564732658974/

Gotlieb, Lori. "How Changing Your Story Can Change Your Life." Filmed September 2019 at TED@DuPont, Philadelphia, Pennsylvania. Video, 16:17. https://www.ted.com/talks/lori_gottlieb_how_changing_your_story_can_change_your_life?language=en

Murphy, Ryan. *Eat Pray Love*. United States: Columbia Pictures, 2010.

Chapter 1

Encyclopædia Britannica. Online Ed. s.v. "Transcendentalism." Accessed April 22, 2021. https://www.britannica.com/event/Transcendentalism-American-movement.

Thoreau, Henry David. "Journal II." 19 August 1851. *Walden*. Accessed April 22, 2021. https://www.walden.org/work/journal-ii-1850-september-15-1851/

Thoreau, Henry David. *Walden: or, Life in the Woods*. London: J. M. Dent, 1908.

Chapter 2

Janzen, Emma. "Day of the Dead Drinking Traditions." *Imbibe Magazine*, October 30, 2017. Accessed April 22, 2021. https://imbibemagazine.com/day-of-the-dead-drinking-traditions/

Mercer, Anne. "Disney World Hidden Mickeys: The Ultimate Hunting Guide." *Tripster*, September 20, 2017. Accessed April 22, 2021. https://www.tripster.com/travelguide/disney-world-hidden-mickeys-ultimate-hunting-guide/

Chapter 3

Williams, Margery. *The Velveteen Rabbit*. London: Egmont Books, 2004.

Chapter 4

Things to do in Jamaica. "Ricks Cafe in Negril, Jamaica." Accessed April 22, 2021 https://things-to-do-in-jamaica.com/ricks-cafe-negril-jamaica/

Chapter 5

Elrod, Hal. *The Miracle Morning: The 6 Habits That Will Transform Your Life before 8 AM.* London: John Murray Learning, 2016.
New 7 Wonders. "Chichén Itzá." Accessed April 22, 2021. https://world.new7wonders.com/wonders/pyramid-at-chichen-itza-before-800-a-d-yucatan-peninsula-mexico/

Chapter 7

Discover Puerto Rico. "Visit El Yunque National Forest." Accessed April 22, 2021. https://www.discoverpuertorico.com/article/visit-el-yunque-national-forest

Chapter 9

Homer. *The Odyssey.* Translated by Robert Fagles. New York: Viking, 1996.

Chapter 10

Columbus, Chris, Howard Shore, Fred Steiner, and Howard Shore. *Mrs. Doubtfire.* United States: Twentieth Century Fox, 1993.
Goleman, Daniel. *Emotional Intelligence: Why It Can Matter More Than IQ.* New York: Bantam Books, 1995.
Torfadóttir, Áslaug. "Elves, Trolls and Monsters." *Iceland Travel* (blog). April 25, 2019. Accessed April 22, 2021. https://www.icelandtravel.is/blog/elves-trolls-monsters-iceland.

Chapter 11

National Aeronautics and Space Administration (NASA) Glenn Research Center. "Newtons Laws of Motion." Accessed April 22, 2021. https://www1.grc.nasa.gov/beginners-guide-to-aeronautics/newtons-laws-of-motion/

Chapter 13

Daniels, Erica, "The Complete Rose Color Meanings Guide." *Proflowers* (blog). Accessed April 22, 2021. https://www.proflowers.com/blog/rose-color-meanings/

Chapter 14

Video Advice. "You Are the Creator. Warning: This Might Shake Up Your Belief System! Morgan Freeman and Wayne Dyer." February 9, 2018. Video, 10.01. https://youtu.be/r7cYsgB4G1s

Chapter 16

Barrett, P. G. "Standing on The Dock Waiting for Your Ship to Come In." *Medium.* December 25, 2019. Accessed October 10, 2021. https://medium.com/swlh/standing-on-the-dock-waiting-for-your-ship-to-come-in-890a7fff5d15